Throwing Fire at the Sun, Water at the Moon

VOLUME 40

Sun Tracks
An American Indian Literary Series

Throwing Fire at the Sun, Water at the Moon

ANITA ENDREZZE

With Illustrations by the Author

The University of Arizona Press
Tucson

First printing
The University of Arizona Press
This book is printed on acid-free, archival-quality paper.
Manufactured in the United States of America

05   04   03   02   01   00   6   5   4   3   2   1

Library of Congress Cataloging-in-Publication Data
Endrezze, Anita.
Throwing fire at the sun, water at the moon / Anita Endrezze ;
with illustrations by the author.
p. cm. — (Sun tracks ; v. 40)
Includes bibliographical references.
ISBN 0-8165-1971-4 (cloth)
ISBN 0-8165-1972-2 (paper)
1. Yaqui Indians Poetry. 2. Indians of Mexico Poetry. 3. Yaqui
mythology. I. Title. II. Series.
PS501 .S85 vol. 40 PS3555.N383
810.0′0054 s — dc21
[818′.5409]
99-6688
CIP

British Library Cataloguing-in-Publication Data
A catalogue record for this book is available from the British Library.

Some of the work presented here has been published before in the
following publications, sometimes in slightly different versions: "A Journey
to the Heart" in *Here First*, edited by Brian Swann (Modern Library,
2000); "Red at Bacum" in *Carolina Quarterly* (vol. 50, no. 1, Fall 1997);
"Coyote Woman" in the anthology *In the Eye of the Deer* (Aunt Lute Press,
1999); "Grandfather Sun Falls in Love with a Moon-Faced Woman" in
Carolina Quarterly (vol. 50, no. 1, Fall 1997); "Lost River" and "My Little
Sister's Heart in My Hands" in *Lost Rivers*, edited by Anthony Selbourne
(Making Waves Press, England, 1997); and "The Humming of Stars and
Bees and Waves" in *Talking Leaves*, edited by Craig Lesley (Dell, 1991).

Publication of this book is made possible in part by the proceeds of a
permanent endowment created with the assistance of a Challenge Grant
from the National Endowment for the Humanities, a federal agency.

Contents

PART ONE

In the Navel of the Moon: Mexico

PART TWO

Cuentos de Mi Familia / Stories of My Family

Illustrations

Acknowledgments

The Artist Trust of Washington provided funds through the GAP Award that allowed me to travel to Sonora, Mexico, homeland of the Yaqui. It was a journey to connect with both the geographical and emotional landscape of my tribe. I would like to thank the trust for its generosity.

Thanks also to the Spokane Art Commission, which presented my paintings (some of which appear in this book) in an exhibit at Chase Gallery, City Hall, Spokane, Washington, in August 1998. Also exhibited were Elizabeth Woody and Gail Tremblay.

I would also like to acknowledge the help of my family, who tried to remember all the old stories, even though none of us could agree on which was the "right" version. Thanks to Barbara, Rondi, Mary Francis, Tim, Raymond—and our mothers. Also, thanks to my aunts, who spoke only in Spanish, and to Mary Francis, who helped me to understand. Gracias.

Both Alan Schroder and Patti Hartmann at the University of Arizona Press provided help in the manuscript phase of this book. Thank you both. In addition, a special thanks to Jane Kepp of Kepp Editorial for her careful reading and editing.

This book is for our children, especially my two: Aaron Joseph Sun Hawk Danielson and Maja Sierra Rose Hansen.

A Journey to the Heart

The faces of my ancestors are both luminous and shadowy. I'm standing in a long line, holding the memory of their hands. My own hands are bone and muscle, sinew and threadlike veins of blood. We're dreaming about each other or maybe playing a game of "telephone," hundreds of years old. You know, where one person whispers a message or story to another, who then whispers it to the next person in line. *Pass it on*. The message is changed, perhaps only slightly but continually, until it has created a new language, a different shape of itself. Or maybe the words become the dimple in your mother's cheek or the stubborn cowlick in your sister's hair. Still, there is a connection of breath, heart, mind, and spirit.

Not one of my immediate ancestors was a professional storyteller, yet all told stories about our families, and collectively the stories of their lives have influenced me.

I'm half Indian and half white. Most people assume it's my mother who is Indian. Not so. My mother's grandparents came from Vinica (Slovenia), Fai Della Paganella (alpine Italy), and Curciu (Romania). For sociopolitical reasons, they all probably spoke German in addition to their national languages. They were two men and two women, traveling individually from their small villages to the end of the earth: Butte, Montana. They came in the late 1890s: Johanna Ostronič, Joseph Kambič, Elizabeth Yaeger, Eugenio Endrizzi.

Like many young men, Eugenio Endrizzi intended to work for a few years in America, make his fortune, and return to Italy. In Butte, he met Elizabeth Yaeger, and they married and had children (my grandfather, William Eugene "Papa Billy," was one of them). Eugenio had already sent his family back to Italy when he was killed in a mining accident on October 11, 1905. He was thirty-eight.

I have a copy of the newspaper article about his death. The headline reads: *Dead*

Miners Careless. Below that it says "Endrizzi and O'Neill failed to follow instructions of the shift boss."

Further headlines add: *Crushed Beneath Tons of Rock in Speculator Mine*.

The detailed article goes on to say that "suddenly and without warning, an immense quantity of rock came down from the hanging wall and caught O'Neill and Endrizzi. One of them spoke a few words after falling, but the other appeared to be dead."

I'd like to think it was my great-grandfather passing on that message, speaking his last few words. What did he say? I'm still listening. Maybe my son was learning as he arranged his rock collection. The beauty of each rock was formed under certain immense pressures in the heart of the earth. Each rock exists, singular in its own beauty, and ageless. Like people.

Eugenio's widow and children returned to that raw city of bricks and trees burnt leafless by the sulfuric acid in the air. Butte was a city of great wealth, vitality, and death. A town that heaved itself up and out of the earth, home to immigrants from Ireland, Italy, Scotland, and Scandinavia. My mother was born there.

Her name is Jean and she is Papa Billy's daughter. She's fair-skinned with amber-colored eyes and blondish brown hair. I have photos of her when she was a little girl, wearing her blond hair in a Dutch-boy haircut. She's told me how she played on the mine tailings.

Shortly before World War II, she moved to Long Beach, California, and worked in the naval shipyards, drafting. She was very good at it. The blue lines were clean, neat, and precise.

My maternal grandmother, Ann, or Nana, was also a quiet woman. Deeply religious, she tried to get me to go to mass. My mother wouldn't let her. Even so, I grew up with ideas and experiences in both Catholic and Protestant churches. Nana was ninety-two when she died in 1994, and she taught me a lot about patience. She was a nurse in a time when nurses were instructed how to formulate their own disinfectants and told how to prepare a kitchen for a woman's birth labor. She was born in Butte, Montana.

She was a good shot; they called her "Annie Oakley." But she was also fearful, didn't like taking risks, avoided changes. I have tried to follow my mother's example of saying yes to life's possibilities. Still, I can understand my grandmother. In her lifetime, the world went through changes tremendous and frightening to the timid soul.

Her husband, my Papa Billy, was a steamfitter by trade and an inventor by inclination. He invented an ore classifier used in the Montana mines.

He had a rock collection: stunning purple crystals and clusters of yellow crystals that caught and refracted the light. We set them all on our mantel. Blue-green rocks—copper—that we were warned not to lick. Solid "fool's gold," or pyrite, which made our childish eyes glitter. Heavy chunks of lead. I learned the names of rocks before I learned my multiplication tables.

Although Papa Billy's father had been killed in that mining accident, he was fascinated with the deep earth—and the deep sea. Papa Billy invented a nuclear-powered submarine with a conical-shaped hull. I still have all his patent drawings. I can see his drafting table, set square in the golden light of a lace-curtained window. Pens. Straightedge. Crumbly erasers. A small penknife to sharpen thin-leaded pencils. The implements of his creativity were just as exciting to me as his creations.

Someday I'd like to write a book about my mother's side of the family.

My father, Alexander Raymond Diaz, was Yaqui. A full-blood with a dark moon face and hair so black it shone blue at times. When he met my mother, he was a divorced motorcycle mechanic for the Long Beach Police Department. After they were married, they tried to buy a house, but because he was Indian, no one would sell one to him. And because my mother was a woman, she wasn't allowed to buy one either.

I wrote about this in "La Morena as the Sad-Eyed Jaguar Priest." La Morena means "the dark woman," and she is one aspect of the female presence in many of the poems and prose poems I have included in this book. I am also related to the Moreno family. My godfather was Alex Moreno (see the poem "Anonymous Is Coyote Girl"). Additionally, the Virgin of Guadalupe is known as "La Morenita," which is an affectionate way of saying "the little dark one," since she is of *indio* blood.

"Someday, your daughter's going to write about this," La Morena promises in "La Morena as the Sad-Eyed Jaguar Priest." "Doesn't matter if she gets it the way it really happened. Nothing happens the way we remember it."

While collecting stories for this book, I asked relatives for their memories and discovered that people remember things differently. One story might be told three different ways, filtered by individual perceptions and by time. I was intrigued by something Stravinsky said: that we live by memory, not by truth. In gathering material for this book, I learned that the truth is not often found in fact. The reporting of history is always subjective, no matter who is telling it. This discovery freed me: I was able to figure out how I wanted to approach my family history—as fact or fiction? Long troubled by the question, I decided to do it in both ways. This book, therefore, is history, myth, family anecdotes, poetry, and short stories, and they are all the same thing.

Yaquis have had centuries of contact with Europeans. The first Spaniard went through in about 1533 on a slave-raiding expedition. Another explorer, Francisco de Ulloa, saw "naked people" and smoke signals on the beach as he sailed up the Gulf of California sometime between 1539 and 1541. There have been periods of relative peace, but consider this: at one time, there were thirty thousand Yaquis living in eighty *rancherías*. Three hundred years later, there were only ten thousand left. For better and for worse, Spanish culture, language, and religion have influenced Yaqui culture.

Other tribes in the region have fared worse. Of the ten original Cahita-speaking tribes, only the Mayos and Yaquis survived.

The Yaquis have lived near the Río Yaqui in northwestern Sonora for thousands of years. In fact, one name given to us is Hia Hiaqui, which means "People Who Shout across the River." Another name used by native speakers is Yoemem. It means "the People."

My father's parents, Carlotta Ramos and Emiterio (Meetah) Diaz, were Yaquis from Mexico. It was a terrible time. Just before my grandparents were born, more than one hundred Yaquis were burned to death in a church in Bacum, one of the eight Yaqui pueblos. This is what happened: six hundred men, women, and children surrendered to a Mexican colonel, who ordered four hundred fifty of them into the church. The others were let go. He kept ten leaders as hostages and promised that if there were any attempts to escape, all hostages would be shot. He trained his artillery on the church door. I tell about this in the poem "Red at Bacum."

There were constant battles against the Mexican government and the soldiers, the *federales*, who enforced the tax collections and took away Yaqui rights and land. Reprisals against the Yaquis included deportation to Yucatán, enslavement, rape, murder, and starvation. My grandfather, Meetah, was just a boy when he saw his father murdered by Mexicans. Meetah escaped by hiding under the porch and later walked north. In "Bones Resembling My Grandfather" I relate how he "scooped up handfuls of mud and made a turban of wet earth" as he crossed the Salton Sea. This is how he avoided sunstroke. Since the Salton Sea wasn't formed until after 1905–1906, when the area was flooded by the releasing of a dike damming the Colorado River, he must have been there after that date.

In 1886, when Carlotta was a child, the Yaquis suffered a defeat at the hands of the Mexican general Carbo, military commander of Sonora. Two hundred Yaquis died and two thousand became prisoners of war. Diseases claimed the lives of many civilian Yaquis. Many Yaquis were settled in the eight pueblos, under the control of the government, but the majority left the Yaqui Valley, seeking work and freedom. Some fled to the rugged Bacatete Mountains. They raided the Mexicans and the pueblo Yaquis.

In 1900, General Torres battled the mountain Yaquis and killed four hundred men. Many others committed suicide by jumping off cliffs. More than a thousand women and children were forced to march down the trail. Most died along the way. This is called the Massacre of Mazocoba. Only eighteen federales were killed and sixty wounded. Thirty-five guns were taken from the Yaquis during the "battle."

By 1907, Yaquis were a cash commodity, selling for sixty pesos a head to the owners of henequen plantations in Yucatán and sugar fields in Oaxaca.

Many Yaquis left Mexico at this time, some fleeing to Arizona, refugees from their homeland, always hoping they would be able to return. My grandparents (separately, since they were not married at this time) went to California.

Although Yaqui history continued hand in hand with Mexican history (in 1910 the Mexican Revolution changed the country), my grandparents had removed themselves from those dangers and begun to merge with American history and culture.

The Arizona Yaquis maintained a more unified identity as a tribal people than did those who lived in California, who blended into a Mexican American identity. My grandparents struggled with making a living and raising children. Although my father grew up knowing he was Yaqui and heard the family stories, he was not political. Even after my parents divorced and he moved to Green Valley, Arizona, he didn't participate in the Yaqui effort to establish a reservation outside of Tucson. Instead, he was busy with his nursery business and raising my two younger half-siblings. In ill health for a number of years, he died in 1979, the same year the Pascua reservation was approved by the federal government.

My grandmother Carlotta Ramos came to the United States before 1916 (when my father was born here)—probably around 1902. An astute businesswoman, she later owned property in several California counties: produce fields and houses for field workers. She carried her money wrapped up in her shawl. My father clearly remembered the early days, when they all had to pick lettuce and strawberries and walnuts in order to survive. They went as far as San Francisco, working in the fields.

Carlotta had been raped by Mexican soldiers. I wrote about it in the poem "Angelina," which appears in Part Two of this book. A bad thing happened to Carlotta, but by all accounts she was a good and kind person. *She* was not the bad thing. She was stronger than that.

Carlotta's father, Pedro Ramos, had been a merchant in Sonora. He had a caravan of burros loaded with supplies that he traded and sold along the coast near Guaymas, Sonora. It is possible that he was also a smuggler, perhaps a gunrunner for the Yaquis in the mountains.

Pedro was murdered, "shot by Mexicans dressed as Indians," according to family legend. This phrase always made me wonder until I learned more about Yaqui history. I think that the mountain Yaquis had a disdain for the pueblo Yaquis and would have characterized them as "Mexicans dressed as Indians." In other words, the pueblo Yaquis may have dressed like other Yaquis but were really Mexican at heart, living and accepting Mexican rule. Or perhaps he was simply shot by Mexican bandits.

In any case, his wife, my great-grandmother Estefana Garica, marched to the local law authority. With a gun on each tiny hip, she demanded that he find the killers or die himself.

Another story is told about her. She had a tooth pulled—and it was the wrong one. She swore she'd kill the "dentist." For more about her, read "Estefana's Necklace of Bullets."

My Yaqui grandmothers were strong women, educated, clever, and fearless. Carlotta was also graceful, exceedingly beautiful, and kind. She fed hoboes, loved music (she played the twelve-string guitar), and sang. She was only four feet, eleven inches tall, with masses of dark hair piled up on top of her head. Her eyes were deep black. I have her photo on my office wall, next to one of her husband, Meetah. He's posed stiffly in a suit, with a shock of unruly hair escaping out from under a dark hat. He didn't like Mexicans. He lived his life like an Indian, he'd say to anyone. He could easily lift four hundred pounds, according to my father. Meetah was five-ten and stocky. As a young man, he trained horses all over California and Arizona. He died from a hit-and-run accident in the middle of the night in Long Beach, California, on September 19, 1937. He'd probably been drinking. I wrote about it in "Grandfather Sun Falls in Love with a Moon-Faced Woman." The story is actually a retelling of an old Yaqui story about the sun falling in love with the moon, but I wove it into our family history.

Meetah owned a junkyard that now is just part of the neighborhood across the street from the Long Beach Community Hospital, where I was born. His was a long journey, from his experience as a boy witnessing his father, Valentino, being murdered by soldiers to the experiences of a man living not far from Hollywood, town of illusions and fantasy.

Valentino also dealt with *his* father's death. Valentino and his brother and father had been up in the mountains in Sonora, hunting for honey, when something happened. I don't know what, maybe a heart attack or a fall down the mountain trail. The boys had to bury their father there among the red rocks and crumbling earth.

Diaz is not a Yaqui name but one given to our family. It is a Mexican name, specifically that of the Mexican president Porfirio Díaz, who was in power from 1876 to 1910. Sometime during that period, we acquired that last name. I was born Anita Diaz. Other family surnames were Flores, Garica, and Ramos—all Mexican names, not Yaqui. Many Yaquis had both a Yaqui name and a Mexican name, along with nicknames by which they were more commonly known. My childhood nickname was "Stormy." My Indian name, given to me shortly after my birth, is Desert Rose.

Life was hard for my ancestors. They didn't live long. But I know about them through the stories we still tell. There are not enough stories; I always want to hear more. I want to understand them and learn more about them and myself. I want my children, Aaron and Maja, to know them also. That's why I write and paint, to *pass it on*.

The history of words is the history of people. People define and are defined by their language. If you study languages, you learn about war, religion, adventure, and spirit. I think it is interesting that scholars studying Indian languages today are coming to realize that the great diversity of languages in this hemisphere supports the idea that we have been here a lot longer than the accepted, academic starting point of 11,500 years ago (the Clovis timetable). Indeed, recent research has agreed that native people have been here for about 45,000 years. The voice of a people truly is their history.

My father never spoke Yaqui. When he was young, he was ashamed of being Indian. He didn't want to listen to the old stories. And yet he liked to tell us about what life was like "in the old days." My younger half-sister, Rondi (who was born in Farmington, New Mexico, on March 15, 1959), told me how our father would go skinny-dipping in the ocean and the police would take his clothes. He traveled with his family in a buckboard wagon into Los Angeles. He was, she says, great at storytelling, funny, and generous. Rondi says, "I see him with both the eyes of an adult and the memory of a child. When I was little, he was wonderful. He'd sing for me and let me blow up the muscles on his arm by blowing hard on his thumbs." But he also ran around with other women and was a "happy drunk." For some time he was separated from her mother, and he lived for a while in New Mexico. We have a picture of him giving a corn grinding demonstration at Chaco Canyon.

Rondi says, "He claimed to be a Catholic. Other times, he'd talk of the Happy

Hunting Grounds. If truth be known, he didn't believe in anything. Whatever served his purpose at the moment." Yet she also relates how he became a Christian later in his life and was a changed person: "He became kind, considerate, and humble." She enjoyed being with him then. "So his last days were his happiest. They were my happiest, also, because I found my dad before he died," she told me.

Our father, Alex, was married three times (my mother was the second) and had six legitimate children plus several illegitimate ones. My older half-sister, Mary Francis, has only good memories of him. She still misses him, twenty years after his death. My full sister, Barbara, remembers him not at all. My other two half-siblings, Raymond and Tim, have mixed feelings about our father.

My parents' marriage was very troubled. We lived for a while in Merlin, Oregon, near Grant's Pass. My parents logged their land. I remember napping in a tent covered with crawling caterpillars. I breathed the close, green-tinted, pine-scented air. I heard the milky sighs of my sleeping baby sister, Barbara.

It was a place of violence, I've since learned. I wrote a poem about it, which appears in this book. It's called "My Little Sister's Heart in My Hands."

I remember my father's violence. He scared me. We finally left, my mother secretly stealing away with us girls. We moved around a lot after that. From birth to age eighteen, I lived in thirteen different houses. I went to a different school every year from sixth to twelfth grade. In the poem "Housing Dreams" (in the recently published *The Humming of Stars and Bees and Waves*) I say, "There's no rhythm / to moving / except the moving." And "we moved / because we were nowhere / better / than tomorrow." For many Indian writers, place is vital. For me, it's been thought and feeling, an emotional landscape. A landscape of dreams and stories. It's been four generations on either side of the family since someone has died where they were born. We have been rootless for more than one hundred years. And yet that restlessness, or desperation for something better, has given us a vitality, a sense of adventure. While I have a Danish husband and my children can find their roots in many countries of the world, we are Americans in the special way in which only those who have Indian blood can connect to this land.

I have just moved to the Seattle area from Spokane, which is a very white city. Fewer than 1 percent of its people are Native American, and fewer than 3 percent Hispanic. There are a couple of Yaquis there, other than my brother Tim's family. I've met several people, including a dentist and a librarian, who say their families came from Sonora or Durango, but they don't know which tribes. Other Indians, some Lakotas and Apaches, for example, have never been to their tribe's homeland. Urban Indians have a problem of identity, especially among the youth. But there's also a sharing of culture that helps to define "Indian." One example of this is powwow dancing. Plains Indian regalia has been adopted by people of many other culture regions. I don't live in a Yaqui community, but I do identify myself as Indian and, more specifically, as Yaqui.

Knowing whether someone is Indian or not may help me find a connection with that person, a sense of familiarity and acceptance, but more important to me is learning whether that person has a good heart. In Yaqui it is said, "Nejpo wa itom jiak Yoemia si tuu jiapsekame." In Spanish it is "Soy la tribu Yaqui de gran corazón." It means "I am the Yaqui tribe of great (good) heart." As an individual Yaqui, that is my goal—to have a good heart, to be kind and loving. It is individuals who make up a tribe and an identity.

Those early ancestors of mine, those "naked people" sending smoke signals from the white beaches to the tattered sails of a creaking Spanish ship, sent the very human message, *We are here* (read the story "Throwing Fire at the Sun"). In the face of the unknown, humans have always left their mark: handprints on cave walls, painted suns on rocks, flute solos to the stars. Sometimes words are inadequate for communication. Elements must be transformed. Mineral pigments into paint. Sound into song. Fire into smoke.

When words fail me, turning as elusive and annoying as smoke, when I need to touch, then I paint or make baskets. I can work with texture and color that become almost immediately visible and tangible. It pleases me to have something I can *touch* after working so much with words and thought. The struggle to put ideas into words is itself important to the formation of a writer's vision and growth. Painting uses a different set of tools (brush, paper, paint, water), but the struggle is still there.

In the Aztec creation myth, Hungry Woman falls from the intangible spirit world and creates the foundations of the world with her body (read "Coatlicue"). We are like her. Our bones are part rock, our hair part grass, and our tears part ocean and human feelings. Our link to the world of animals and plants and minerals is one we should never forget. We are also like her in that we struggle to make our spiritual values and intellectual concepts into the physical reality of this world.

In the Yaqui story of creation, Yomumuli creates everything out of love and joy. She guides both people and animals and offers them free will within a set of moral laws. Those humans who can't accept her prophecy of the future are free to leave and go into the desert or the sea, where they become ants or dolphins. But it is said that if you are lost at sea, the dolphins will help you back to land because they remember the time when we were all one people. And if you are lost in the desert, the ants will also help you, remembering the time when we were all related.

I have included different versions of the Yomumuli creation story in this book to show that fragments of the old stories survive and tantalize us with the mystery of their lost wholeness. *Yomumuli* means "enchanted bee." Since bees are primarily female, this could suggest that early Yaqui society was matrilineal. There's another story that starts out with the focus on the male but soon changes back to two girls: a man named Yomomuli had twin daughters. He was asked by the elders to interpret the Talking Tree but couldn't, nor did he think his daughters would be able to do any better than he. But they went to the sea and spoke to a fish (perhaps a dolphin), whereupon they gained the knowledge necessary to interpret. In all the versions of Yomumuli, the humming sound is important. The tree hums, but the female has a name that also hums: enchanted bee. Sound is a connection between the old ways and the new, a translation of the spiritual into words/breathe/sound, and a link between myth and what will become history. The talking tree or stick may be found in several places in Yaqui country; for example, near Vicam there is an ancient volcanic mountain called Omteme Kawi (Angry Mountain). Nowadays, it has a microwave tower on it.

I recently made a pilgrimage. Thanks to Artist Trust, an arts organization in Washington State, I was able to travel to Sonora, Mexico. The grant covered my costs and I traveled lightly, eating one big meal a day (shrimp or fish soup with lobster fresh from the sea), walking with my day pack along the highways, flagging down buses. I hiked along miles of white sandy beaches, rode a horse into the desert, and entered the warren of small shops in the old shopping district of Guaymas. Everywhere, I looked for faces I would recognize. Faces of people who might look like relatives. And I found them, on street corners selling oranges, riding the buses, driving taxis. In my broken Spanish, I told everyone I spoke to that my grandparents came from here, that I was a Yaqui. And they all smiled, welcoming me. We talked about the ancient red mountains, the turquoise sea, the fields of strawberries. I saw the Bacatete Mountains, where my great-grandfather died. I saw Bacum. I saw Vicam. I saw the Río Yaqui as it flowed toward the sea through fields of maize. On its banks was a restaurant called the Río Yaqui selling Tecate beer and seafood.

I wrote the short story "A Good Journey Home to Vicam" after I returned.

Another story, "The Walking Stone," also takes place in modern Guaymas but is based on an old Yaqui folktale. Both of these stories are included in this book.

I took lots of photos. Once home I began painting: interpreting vision and symbol and reality. In the visual section of the book, I'm synthesizing experience with art, preparing to pass on my ideas to others. My trip to our tribal homeland was a journey to the heart.

PART ONE

In the Navel of the Moon

Mexico

The original pre-Hispanic name for Mexico
was Mexica (pronounced *meh-SHEE-ka*). It means
"in the navel of the moon" and refers to the
similarities between the lake that Mexico City is
built on and the shape of the rabbit in the moon.
Mexicans who came to the United States called
themselves *mexicanos*, hence the word *chicano*.
Another term used to define those of mixed *indio*
and European ancestry is *mestizo*. I could call
myself chicana, una mestiza, Yaqui.

Other names for Yaqui are Hia Hiaqui, which
means "People Who Shout across the River," and
Yoemem, or "the People."

The Gulf of California

There are two memories of tides:
one for the deep blackness that split
away from the mother sea
and one for sea that found itself
in the daybreaks of rivers.
Yet it was all one sea
tracked by comets and the Elegant Tern,
seals in speckled pod-shaped skins,
and whales, opening their small eyes
when the hands of people drew fish
out of the salt.

Geologists tell us that the sea split
millions of years ago
before the Yoemem, Yoremem,
Kunkaak, O-Otam [1]
curled their tongues around the names
of themselves and raised the conch shell
to their lips, so that the sound of nature
became human, too:

kalifornia vaawe

Then the sea was measured
and divided into leagues.
The Spanish ships called it *dangerous*
because the sea tore in two ways,
tide and rivers,
so they contained it in maps
written on dead animal skins
with ink made from dried octopus blood

Mar de la Kalifornia
Golfo de California

Then it was named the *Vermilion Sea*
when the red-shelled crabs clicked in the waters.
It was named the *Sea of Cortés*
because it's the right of the Conqueror
to claim the world in his name.

It's his right to name hunger after himself
and to take away rivers
and children
and to give back the bare bones
of life
in the Queen's name.

What can you say about men
who name the mountains "mother"
madre
when the worst curse they can shout
defiles their mother
in the act of creation?

Now we call the Gulf of California
polluted
with the pesticides of fields
and the wastes of factories.
And the voices of the fin-backed whale,
sardines, sea-kelp, anemone,
and turtle are quieter,
so that we have less memory
of the way it was
and less hope
for the way it will be.

In the winter I eat strawberries
from Mexico
and oranges, sectioned and split
apart
on my north continental plate.
I don't know much about my relatives
picking the fields near Bacum, Torim.

I don't know much about the spiny sea urchin,
except that it knows more than I
about the sea, the sea that names itself
unnameable
movable horizon.

The Female Soul of Mexico

It's been said that Mexico has a female soul, that God is a woman in the land of the mestizo (mixed-blood, indio and European). Not only is the spiritual female, but so is the physical manifestation of that spirit. In the land of Aztec war gods and conquistador war dogs, it is the female principle that has prevailed in the concept of the Virgin of Guadalupe.[1]

In 1531, a vision appeared to don Juan Diego, an Indian who believed in the old ways of the Aztecs. He may have been an elder within the Aztec religious institutions before Cortés crushed that civilization.

Before dawn one December morning, Juan Diego walked near the hill of Tepeyacac, where stones were set among flowers. He saw a beautiful woman wearing a turquoise *rebozo*, or mantle, and a rose-colored dress. She encouraged him to have a temple built on the hill where previously the Aztec goddess Tonantzin had been worshipped.

The vision spoke to him in Nahuatl. He stared, wide-eyed, and wondered, "Am I awakening? Where am I? Perhaps I am now in the terrestrial paradise which our elders had told us about?"[2]

The woman spoke: "Juanito, Juan Dieguito." Her clothes were glowing like the sun, the ground around her shone with glitter, and her body emanated a special light.

This first account of the apparition of a spirit woman was written in Nahuatl in 1549 and not translated into Spanish for another hundred years. That it was written in the native language is important, because it shows the origin of La Virgen. Her Nahuatl name, Tequatlasupe, became Guadalupe in Spanish. Her origin, the hilltop called Tepeyacac, was nowhere near the town of Guadalupe in Spain. Not geographically, not spiritually. She called herself the Mother of God, and she was in the Aztec family of gods and goddesses. The Spaniards took her as their own, as a

Christian Mary. But she was more than that and different. Our Lady of Guadalupe has dark skin and European features. She is the first Mother of the Mestizos, the mother of modern Mexico, and her name has been the battle cry of independence for Mexicans and indios for centuries. Her shrines are found on roadsides and in family altars and yards. *She is the Mother of the People.*

According to the writer Gloria Anzaldúa, she is the three mothers of the Chicano people.[3]

She is Guadalupe, who never abandoned us. She represents a continuation of history and spirit, a bridge between cultures.

She is also Malinche, the woman who represents all indias who have been sold, raped, and have borne mestizo children.[4] Until chicana feminists understood and fought for Malinche, she was abandoned by the people.

The last of the three mothers is La Llorona, the Crying Woman. She seeks all her lost children everywhere, in the alleys of the barrios, in the desert, in the skyscrapers of the City of Angels. La Llorona is the raped woman whose children have abandoned her; she is the raped woman who slew her own children; she is the dark face of the Eater of Filth, another Aztec goddess. She is the mourning woman who determinedly kills men with her beauty. She is revenge, destruction, a Mexican version of Kali.

I would like to give you some background on the poems that follow this essay on the female soul of Mexico.

"Coatlicue" is a poem that can be read horizontally or vertically. That is, you may read it from left to right or in two separate columns up and down. The left-hand column tells one Aztec version of creation. Hungry Woman is a spirit woman, first only a thought in the universe. But as she thinks about life, she conceives herself. She becomes a body with mouths. She is hungry for life. The spirit world can no longer contain her. She falls to earth, where her body becomes our planet.

The right-hand column tells another Aztec version of creation. The Lady of the Serpent Skirt becomes pregnant by a phallic object, a knife. It is an obsidian knife—stone made from volcanic glass, once molten from the earth's womb. She gave birth to the universe, again always hungry for life and its necessity, death. Her skirt was made of skulls and snakes. All over the world, snakes are respected for their ability to go to the underworld and to renew themselves as they shed their skins.

The Lady of the Serpent Skirt became pregnant again and gave birth to the war god. He destroyed all her other children and killed his own mother.

This story may have some historical truth to it. Perhaps it tells about a dynasty that self-destructed, or about a family who murdered one another for the sake of power. The Greek myths and legends are full of such violence.

In "Mother of the Lord of Near and Far," the first stanza describes the Virgin of Guadalupe, but as you will see, she seems to be very native. When an Aztec woman was pregnant, she wore a black sash around her middle. So does the Virgin.

The second stanza describes her standing on a black crescent moon, crushing the head of a snake (which, according to Christian authorities, represents the crushing of Aztec culture). The moon, however, has long been a female symbol, because its cycle so closely parallels our menstrual cycle. And the snake has also been associated with women: Eve's temptation, women priestesses who used snakes (and their hallucinogenic venom) for telling the future, and the snake as a symbol of healing and regeneration. The complexities of symbols—both Christian and non-Christian—reveal the breadth of human search for spirit.

The eagle has always been held in reverent regard by native people on this continent. The eagle, flying high, is closer to God. An eagle feather is sacred. Not only did the United States adopt the eagle as its national (and now protected) bird, but the eagle is central to Mexican history as well. According to legend, the ancestors of the Aztecs wandered south to the center of Mexico. They looked for a sign that would tell them where to settle. They traveled for a long time, until one day they saw an eagle sitting on a cactus. The bird was devouring a snake. This was the sign, and there they stayed, to build a civilization, found a nation, and create one of the great cities of the world, Tenochtitlán, now Mexico City.[5]

The long poem "Corn Mother" starts with the image of a lake below present-day Mexico City. The city is actually built over the ancient marshes and lake, which was channeled and bridged by the Aztecs. Floating gardens once provided food and flowers for the native people. The conquistadores were astonished at the beauty of the city. There was nothing like it in Europe. It was clean and safe. Lawlessness was not tolerated. For example, drunk Aztec nobles were executed. Vast markets displayed a bewildering variety of strange food: pyramids of soft cornmeal, baskets of potatoes, mounds of tomatoes.

But if you could go even further back into history, you would find those small grains of grass that became maize, or corn. Twenty thousand years ago corn was harvested and cultivated. Women were the first agriculturists in many parts of the world. In Mexico, the tiny kernels of corn were carefully encouraged to develop into sweeter, juicier food. By A.D. 1200, corn cultivation had reached Canada.

Maize was usually planted with two other crops: beans and squash. The beans provided the nitrogen the corn needed; the cornstalks supported the bean and squash vines. Native people called this trio of crops the "three sisters," adopting them into the human family. Different types of corn were developed to survive the varied climates of two continents.[6]

Following the poem about our corn mother are two versions of the Yaqui creation story. The spirit woman is called Yomumuli. She is gentle and wise, a good mother. She seems worlds away from the Aztec belief system. "Yomumuli and the Talking Tree" is my retelling of the traditional story. Many Yaqui storytellers focus on the message of baptism into Christianity, but since I'm not a Christian, I've omitted that part. The story of the Talking Tree is the Yaqui national story. Because it is from the oral tradition, it has changed throughout the centuries. Some of it has probably been lost. New elements have been added, such as the "metal snake," which is a modern train. But it still holds our imagination and spiritually connects us.

In "The Flower Women," I've added details about Yaqui ways, which I had to learn while writing this. I didn't grow up in a household where I learned that ground-up green corn silk mixed with other herbs and blown into an ear can relieve earache. My version recounts the basic story with poetic embellishments: a tree made of flowers, a tree made of bee eyes, a tree like the spine of a human. But all the "facts" about healing herbs are true of Yaqui remedies. The two women also appear in traditional versions; I've simply given them personalities.

Yaquis absorbed Christian beliefs in unique ways. If you read "An Introduction to Fundamental Interactions," you'll see that although the cultures clashed, they also intertwined.

The next piece, "The Flood," is a retelling, in poem form, of two versions of bad weather. The Río Yaqui is a desert river with its origin in the mountains. Flash flooding is not unknown. The first part of the poem tells about a drought. The people sought divine help from Yuku, god of the rain, and his wife, who provided the rain. The Yaqui people's agent was a magical frog named Bobok (it sounds like a frog's voice). He managed to get up to the sky house where Yuku lived and bring back some rain.

Now the desert flowered, "orange poppies exploding with light / showers of petals flooding the earth."

In the second part, a hybrid version of Yaqui and Christian beliefs, Noah comes to Sonora. He comes to build a boat that can withstand a huge flood. It happened, according to Yaqui oral tradition, on February 17, A.D. 614. The rain fell, and everyone crowded onto the boat. Those who wanted to be Christian stayed aboard; those who didn't jumped overboard and became "animals." What I found especially interesting was learning about those who were stranded on small hills above the receding waters. They were a strange and motley group, definitely a glimpse into the contemporary concept of "magic realism" in storytelling: Emac Dolores—a woman who turned into stone—an angel named Domicilia, and seven birds and seven donkeys. God even talks to everyone. When the people ask for glory, he says, "Drink from the glass from which I drink." After that, none was thirsty—and for a desert people, it was quite a blessing.

In "The Red Rose," Mary lives in Sonora. She finds a red rose by the watering hole and tucks it into her bodice, the same way the Lady of the Serpent Skirt tucked a ball of feathers between her breasts. Both become pregnant by this action. Whereas the Lady, who wore skulls, conceived a war god who beheaded her, Mary conceives a different kind of god who is born from a rose, symbol of female sexuality and love. In the story, I've added more details from my research about the early Yaqui concept of Jesus.

A humorous story, "Jesus as Hopul Woki (Folded Feet)," concludes with the information that although the Christian cross is considered male, Yaquis call it "Our Mother Most Holy Cross," a distinction of some importance.

Throughout this book, I have pulled the threads of the female spirit. From the hungry-mouthed Aztec goddess to the gentle Yomumuli to the character of Sewa in the first Yaqui-European encounter, I knew more stories about my female relatives than about my grandfathers. And even when something happened to a grandfather, it was the woman's point of view that I heard.

In Part Two, "Cuentos de Mi Familia / Stories of My Family," you will meet Coyote Woman—a *bruja*, or witch—the fictitious Esperanza sisters, my grandmother Estefana's necklace of bullets, the moon-faced woman who seduces my grandfather, and the other, mainly female, members of my family, who are both real, mythical, tribal, urban, and imagined from my viewpoint as a writer.

There are motifs that recur throughout this book: bees, snakes, skulls, strong women, butterflies, La Morena, the Virgin. They appear not only because they are part of Yaqui and chicano culture but also because they are world archetypes. They connect people with the time when we were, perhaps, all dreaming the same dream. Time is like a necklace with small fetishes strung on it: jade snakes, indigo butterflies, clay statues of goddesses. The necklace is passed from mother to daughter. The story behind each fetish may be lost over time, but the meaning is always understood.

The last story in Part Two is called "The Humming of Stars and Bees and Waves" and is, again, a retelling of the Yomumuli myth. In this story, the past is interwoven with the present. The end of the story is the future: such is prophecy. It completes the cycle.

Coatlicue

AN AZTEC CREATION STORY IN TWO VERSIONS

Hungry Woman
lived in the universe
of thought
at each wrist, ankle, knee,
shoulder, elbow
she had mouths
she was always hungry
and her spirit helpers
fed her stars, whole
galaxies of red planets,
shooting comets with iridescent tails,
small pockmarked moons,
black holes the size of walnut shells,
suns and more suns, handfuls
of fire and ice
she was hungry

Finally her spirit helpers threw her out,
over the edge of what was known,
and as she fell she invented
what she was falling into:
life, here, this world
upon impact, she sank deeply
into herself, her hair becoming the grass,
her breasts the mountains,
her bones the stones,
her tears the shores of
earthly waters

And when we die
we are consumed
by her again:
Hungry Woman
and the thousand mouths

Lady of the Serpent Skirt
impregnated by an obsidian knife
she gave birth to daughter moon
stars   everywhere sons who were
stars
she wore a skirt of snakes
and skulls, chopped-off hands
were her hungers   life
cosmos
and then one day
she found a ball of feathers
multicolored
which she tucked between her breasts
of monolithic time
until she noticed
she was pregnant again

Her children wanted to throw her out
but not before she gave birth again:
the fiery god of war Huitzilopochtli
a serpent of flames
he destroyed them all
when he beheaded her, mother-creator
destroying
everything
as she fell
dismembered self-contained
in the abyss

Since we were born from catastrophe
by murder and violence
our bones will be scattered
into the skirts
of Coatlicue

Mother of the Lord of Near and Far

She is here, under the shadow
of life. She is her own answer
within a mantle of winter roses,
surrounded by 139 sun spears
and Mexican stars. She is pure
mestizo, wearing the black sash
of pregnancy over the skirt of serpents,
Tonantzin, the dark-faced goddess
with the murderous son.

And she is Tequatlasupe,
Our Lady of Guadalupe,
standing on a black crescent moon,
crushing the head of a snake.
She Who Comes Flying Through
the Night Like an Eagle of Fire,
Tlecuahlacupeuh,
O Madre! always near,
La Morena, morenita,
our little dark one,
the female with a thousand mouths,
la hermana
who looks out of your mirror
with lips bright as red
hearts and divines from your eyes
the twin burnings of your soul.

Corn Mother

Beneath Mexico City, there is a lake
sealed tightly below concrete boulevards
and buildings of blind glass
windows where the pigeons batter their wings
and the cleaning women press damp cloths,
dreaming of the lake beneath the city, where skulls
have been crushed into mud and the long pathways
out of the palaces, the markets where the ripe fruit rotted,
the tables where the pots of chocolate tipped over,
unattended, bone ladles clinking to the floor,

where are we? stories above
the lake and the dead Aztecs
who were kinsmen of the Yaquis,
in some northern desert way,
and I won't pause because history didn't,
if you know your history: you know
that Cortés killed thousands of people,
by sword   hunger   sickness
and all their bones fell into the lake,
the water of floating gardens.

So drill into the sediment
and this is what you'll find:
jade flute music, bamboo combs,
a woman's shy whisper.
Small clay statues:
a woman giving birth,
a hunchbacked old man,
royal seals with jaguars
and jugglers.

Drill deeper to the core:
these are the grasses,
teosinte, Gramineae, zea mays,
maize, corn.

Twenty thousand years ago the seeds
inherited the hands of women.

They cultivated the shaggy heads,
the sacred ears, so that humans
became the same flesh.

6500 B.C.
They sifted the soil across Mexica,
and gave corn a family:
the three sisters
maize
beans
squash

Maize journeyed to Ontario, Canada,
before A.D. 1200.

blue corn
yellow corn
white corn
black corn

Table #1
Corn: endosperm, germ, pericarp, tip cap.
16% moisture (rain, sweat, prayers)
72% starch (sun, moon, fingerprints)
10% protein (Indian flesh, Corn Mother, the virgin of Guadalupe)

zinc: good for your immune system
iron: improves your blood, whether full-blood, mestizo, or Other
aluminum, phosphorous, potassium, boron: chant these minerals
like a prayer, with both hands folded over the earth

Blue corn: tortillas, piki (paper bread
you can write on with the hieroglyphics of your teeth),
chaquegue (cornmeal mush)
atole (cornmeal drink)
corn flakes, syrup,
chips for salsa,

muffins, popcorn
pancakes
polenta

Table #2:
set plates the color of polished sun
for the three sisters

one loves to eat corn on the cob slathered with butter,
sprinkled with salt.
She props her elbows on the table, leans over the plate
and grins, corn sticking between her teeth

one loves to eat spoonfuls of yellow squash
Later, she takes the dried gourd and carves out a door,
like the mouth of a woman surprised in the dark window
as a lover plays a jade flute,
and she hangs the gourd up, in a willow,
so that small brown birds nest
and sleep
warm in the belly of a sister

and one loves to cook beans
as she sings away the day's complaints:
red, black, white, pinto, kidney, green,
lima, butter, navy, pole, frijole,
spotted, striped,
all snap like Nahuatl vowels.

Set the table for the corn mother and her family: Alamo,
Utton, Curry, Santa Ana, Taos
Rose, Best, Average, Yellow, White,
Kinsman.

To prepare corn: Boil it in lime
(it dissolves flesh and bone)
and water ancient as language.
Steep
overnight
while the moon is

an Aztec calendar
dividing centuries
into the green silk body
of the Virgin of Guadalupe,
her chocoatl sex,
her serpent-skirted hips,
her yellow teosinte heart.
In the morning,
take two dark reeds,
pounded into paper,
and using ink from beans,
write poems about maize
then throw out
the liquid.

Rinse, discard
the splattered
blood of innocent
cracked kernels.

Drain, wash, drain.
Grind with stone
in a bowl made of skulls,
grind for five hundred years
until the flour is fine
as Indian bones
and shape into hands,
brown faces, virgins
and mothers,
small icons of corn women
carrying bags of groceries
in Los Angeles, Guaymas,
Spokane, Portland, Seattle.

Yomumuli and the Talking Tree

In the time of *yo ania*, the enchanted world, there were spirits as beautiful as red feathers, and one of them was Yomumuli, whose name means Enchanted Bee. She created everything from her blue-starred fingers: the ocean, the mountains, the animals, and the people. Her favorite people were the tiny Surem. They lived in a village and were almost happy.

In the middle of the village was a tall tree. It made a humming noise. They knew it was important for them to understand the tree, but they couldn't. It was only noise to them, not a voice.

The Surem argued. Why was this tree so important? What was its purpose? Why should they waste all their time trying to figure out what a tree had to say? And why was Yomumuli doing this to them?

She came to them and sighed. They had cross faces and deep down-turned mouths. Their hands were quick and full of anger. They lifted their chins defiantly.

"I'll tell you what the tree is saying," she promised. "But you must believe me."

Everyone nodded and sat down around the tree. She stood next to it and cocked her head, listening. From the desert and mountains, the animals journeyed to join them and stood behind the people, listening.

The tree told them, she said, that they must live in harmony and live according to their kind. The cougar could eat the deer. The snake could eat the rabbit. The deer and rabbit could eat the green growing leaves, and the river could gnaw at the earth until it filled its mouth with the salt of the sea. The animals listened and believed. They left knowing the order of life.

Then Yomumuli told the tree's prophecies. "Someday, strange people will come and all will be changed. You will speak differently. You will cover your breasts with cloth and kneel in stone houses. There will be metal snakes with smoke coming out of the tops of their heads and they will steal you away. Your children will not know you, and the dry earth will be wet with your blood."

The Surem widened their eyes. This was too terrible! Some covered their ears with their hands, and their shell bracelets sounded like the clatter of bones. Others stood up and crossed their arms. They didn't believe Yomumuli, this woman made of corn and moon, this woman made with the soft red light of the earth.

She looked at them, their stiff shoulders and frightened eyes. Shaking her head, she left, walking toward her favorite river, rolling it up and tucking it under her arm. She climbed up a rainbow and no one saw her again, until she was only a story told around the fire.

Some of the Surem left, too, walking deep into the desert. Walking to the horizon, becoming darker and smaller and redder and smaller, until they became ants. They say that if you get lost in the desert, they will help you find your way back because they remember the time when we were all one people.

Other Surem left the village and turned their worried faces toward the sea. They became dolphins and fish-people and whales. They say that if you're lost at sea, they will help you find your way back because they remember the time when we were all one people.

The Surem who decided to stay in the village with their domed houses made of willows and the clay bowls for water and rabbit stew believed Yomumuli and knew that life was a secret language to be learned—and bitter though it would be on the tongue, it was the language of humans.

The Flower Women

Before the Talking Tree, *kutanokame*, the Surem lived in the enchanted world. They neither died nor were sick. Each month when the moon rose full and gravid, they were renewed. The Surem were a small people who lived with nature, understanding the pipe cactus and the frog. In those days, everyone understood a common language, even though it need not be spoken aloud.

The Surem had a leader named Watachomokame. His name meant "he who wears a basket headdress." He knew how to take up a lake, fish and all, and roll it like a rug. He carried it under his arm as the Surem traveled from place to place. He would give the Surem mats of water, folded up like deer hides. This was in the old days, and we used to have a map of the enchanted world then, but we've lost our way.

In Surem, *yo'omuli* means the name of a forest. *Yo* is the way of saying something old or respected.

One day, the Surem discovered a tree in the forest. It was vibrating. The Surem felt that vibration in their spines, tingling up their backs into their minds. The sound was feeling and noise. It was a message, but they couldn't understand it.

The wise men suggested they ask Sea Hamut (a wise woman or a flower woman) if she would help them. She lived in a wild place, a forest full of owls and shadows that danced like deer.

At sunrise, the men journeyed to her home in the mountains. It was a long walk, but the men had purpose in their hearts, so the trip went quickly.

When they reached her house, a mountain lion roared. He was tied up on her porch, where she was sitting, weaving a straw awning for the ramada. Sea Hamut spoke to the lion quietly and the big cat blinked, then sat down, staring at the visitors.

"Lios em chania, mala," greeted the men. God aid you, mother.

She replied, "Lios en chiokoe, hapchim." God forgive you, fathers.

She poured them all drinks of cool water and they sat down. She noticed one of them wincing as he stretched out his leg.

"I'm old," he smiled wryly, "and this knee is stiff."

Sea Hamut got up and went into her house. When she returned she carried a small cup of liquid made from *huchahko* wood. She offered it to the man, who drank it gratefully. It would ease the pain and stop the tiredness in his old muscles. He sighed and handed the cup back to her.

"I wouldn't mind flying back home," joked another man, referring to the feeling of energy and lightness the wood often gave to the person ingesting it.

Sea Hamut smiled and brought out more little cups and a large bowl of the drink. Then, as the men sipped, she listened to their request.

"Only you are wise enough to help us," they concluded. Sea Hamut looked off into the distance. She was old and it was a long way to their town. Even with the *huchahko* wood drink, she wouldn't be able to walk so far.

"I'm sorry," she said. "I'm too old."

The wise men sat quietly, disappointed.

Sea Hamut cleared her throat, and they looked up. She wore a grass skirt with small seashells tied to the ends so that as she stood up, the shells tinkled against her knees. Across her chest she wore an open-arm shirt of soft deer hide, decorated with paint in shapes of moons and stars and whirls like the wind. On her wrinkled cheeks were two blue circles, tattoos. She pointed to the edge of her fields.

A young woman walked with a large deer slung across her shoulders. She was a strong woman with black eyes and hair cut straight across, like the night when it falls into the ocean.

"This is my daughter, who is also Sea Hamut. She will go with you."

The daughter stopped, startled by her mother's words and the sight of strange men. She had never seen men before. She was used to the ways of the forest and the animals. She talked to the morning star, *machi choki*, and she knew how to burn deer bones into chalk or powder and ease body aches with a poultice of the ashes. She knew that ground-up green corn silk mixed with tobacco and *chiltipiquin* (a tiny red berry) cured an earache when it was blown into the ear and the ear was then plugged up with a piece of wild cotton. She knew how to hunt and dress her kill, but she didn't know how to act with people. She stood silently and listened to her mother.

"I've taught my daughter all the wise ways of many worlds, the night world, *tuka ania*, the dream world, *tenku ania*, the way of healing, the way of listening, and the ways of the deep forest, *po cho'oria*. She will go with you and tell you about the Talking Tree."

The young Sea Hamut didn't want to leave her mother, but she agreed to accompany the men. They all rested and then set out the next day. As they left, the lion roared farewell and the young woman ran back. She knelt in front of the lion and rubbed his head between his ears. Then she rose swiftly and jogged back to the wise old men waiting at the edge of the forest.

It was a long trip back to the town, but Sea Hamut never tired. She was strong and wise. At night, when they camped, she guarded the men while they slept. She was never afraid of a new forest because it was all part of her understanding. At last they reached the end of their journey. The town was in sight when Sea Hamut stopped and took out a beautiful dress her mother had given her for the occasion. While she dressed and combed her hair, one of the old men continued into town to announce their arrival.

The town people came out to meet her, expecting to see an old woman, back bent and leaning on a bamboo cane. Instead they saw a well-muscled young woman staring at them. Some of the women came close to Sea Hamut, the Flower Woman, and tried to hug her, but she jumped back and raised her spear. Sea Hamut thought they were attacking her. She growled like a lion.

The old men explained to her their customs of greeting people. After a moment of silence, she nodded and relaxed. She followed them to the Talking Tree.

It was a tall tree, one with flowers of all colors. One without flowers, branches naked and stark. It was a tree made of green corn silk. It was a tree with the small eyes of bees. It was a tree like the spine of a human. It was a tree of spiritual mystery.

Sea Hamut listened. A great part of wisdom is in the listening. She began to understand the Talking Tree. She told them that one day in the future, new men would come. They would bring God and seeds for cultivating. She told them that a new thing would come: death. All would now die and go back into the earth. This death was a payment for the life Earth had given to each and every creature or plant.

When she finished, there was a buzzing confusion among the people. Some people didn't want to accept her words and decided to leave. A great feast of farewell was prepared for them. They danced and ate and said good-bye to their families and friends. When they left they went into the ground and became ants. Where they danced, nothing has ever grown since.

Yet it's a strange thing, because the Surem who left to become ants didn't want to work hard in the fields, clearing stones and planting seeds. But now, as ants, they are the hardest-working insects of all, and they eat seeds and build tunnels. They gave up being human, being Yaqui, although they can understand Yaqui. So you have to be careful what you say around them.

Note: There are several versions of the Yomumuli story, including one in which a father called Yomumuli has twins who help out the people. Twin hero stories are common in the American Southwest.

Similar stories are told all over the world. For example, India has its own version of a Talking

Tree. It is an oracular tree that speaks in every language. The trunk is made of winding snakes. On the boughs, animal heads blink and breathe. The fruits are actually singing women. It is a tree of female divinity.

The Christian Bible tells us about its tree of life and knowledge and the consequent dispersal of humans into the animal world, away from the spirit-filled garden of Eden. In the Yaqui version, people are given free will to choose their destiny without incurring wrath from a spirit being. And most Yaquis believe that this world is also full of spirit and beauty, so that we were not "cast out" into a cursed life.

In most Native American cultures, if you hold the Talking Stick you have permission to speak your mind without interruption.

An Introduction to Fundamental Interactions

Time is not absolute but depends on the direction of the relative motion between two observers making the time measurements.

For example, Event A (the birth of Jesus) may occur before or after Event B (the conquest of Mexico by Europeans), depending on the relative motion of observers making the measurements of time. Depending on the way stars are laid down, like pebbles, in an astronomer's hand. Depending on whether the feathered priest counts the moon or the sun to bundle time in reeds of fifty-two-year cycles. Depending on whether the calendar is named after an emperor whose image is stone, a sarcophagus for his timeless soul.

If the two observers occupy different cultural space, mythically, intellectually, or spiritually, but the same material or physical space, then cultures collide and time explodes.

So Observer A (Yaqui) stands in a field of newly harvested corn, surrounded by canaries and deer. He measures the spirit of Observer B (the slave procurer and explorer Guzmán), who is eyeing the silver knob on the Yaqui's staff of authority. Guzmán has no knowledge of the value of the yellow corn piled in woven willow baskets. He has never seen corn before. He doesn't see people in terms of their beliefs but as muscle power to portage ore samples or carry heavy burdens. His motion is forward at all times: forward to silver, gold, land, slaves. Forward to exploitation and exploration.

The Yaqui, however, tends to view motion as a center from which all movement radiates. He faces Guzmán without understanding that Guzmán values the stone field markers no more than he values the humans in front of him. In fact, Guzmán gives more respect to the markers of property than to the people spread out before him, wearing shells and vivid tattoos. The Yaqui doesn't realize, though he suspects, that Guzmán is changing the motion of Yaqui culture forever by this one encounter on the time line.

So you may read a story of Mary's conception happening before the Jesuits came to the Yaquis, and you may be surprised to read that Jesus walked the paths between the Yaqui *rancherías*. In a way, this is Yaqui revisionist history. It is also a way for the Yaquis to become part of the same time continuum. Yaquis believed in the four directions; time is the fourth dimension. Maybe Einstein was part Yaqui.

This is physics, Native American style.

The Flood

SONORA, MEXICO

1

There was no water, rocks
dried up. People swallowed
the brown skins of mud
lizards, sucked on their knuckles,
bent over the shadow
of a withered moon.
Where was Yuku, lord
of the rain, with his blue skin
and fists that beat terrible
passages into the green clouds?

The People sent a sky sparrow
who flew up into the dry air,
his feathers turning brittle.
"Yuku, send rain!" he implored,
and Yuku assented.
Then the wind came, following
the raw roar of itself, gathering
into a throat of wind, whirling,
the way a cat chasing its own tail
creates furry flashes of sparks.

And at the center, the still
small bird, one eye looking
at the vines of a hurricane,
the trumpeting wind belling,
and the other eye looking
at the end of himself,
his last feather,

a small rafter
bracing the air stuttering
with tiny bones.

So no rain came.
The Yaquis sent a swallow
to Yuku. "Rain!" cried the swallow.
"So it will be," said Yuku.
But under the soft blue belly
of the sky, there were claws
of lightning, and the sky turned over
and over. Wind skinned
the swallow, and the tiny heart
was like nothing you will ever
gather in your dry palms.

There was no rain. No water
fell. Then the Yaquis remembered
the toad, Bobok, who lived in *bahkwam*,
which means "lagoon"
and is now pueblo Bacum.
They begged him to go to Yuku.
"Tomorrow," he promised.

He hurried to his friend
who knew magic.
There, toad took the wings of a bat,
wrapping black folds around him,
and magic saw its own way
over the pimpled skin of toad
and into the flaccid white throat
and down the long thighs
that wiggled in mud.
Then Bobok was bat,
with his leathery wings
and all the wisdom ways
of a dark moon
sleeping head down
under a pale branch.

Bobok flew to Yuku.
"Have pity. Send rain."
Yuku smiled, "Of course!
Rain will follow you."

Bobok cloaked himself
and stepped over the lintel
of Yuku's lodge, where the sky
gleamed and pecked and polished.
Bobok hid under the packed earth,
the exact spot where Yuku stepped out
and in, where the wet toe prints of his wife
shone, and Bobok sniffed
the burned air spoor
of their son-in-law,
the yellow-haired dwarf Suawaka
who throws harpoons of fire
across the sky.
  Bobok hid
while the lightning flooded
the sky and Yuku thundered.
Rain fell: it was Yuku's wife
unsnarling her hair, casting long eyes
at the brimming stems
of clouds. She twisted her hands,
rain fell. Where was Bobok,
who should be choked
in her strong hands?
She raced along the top of wind;
Bobok escaped in the rain
of her hair, crying:
kowak, kowak, kowak.

Rain churned, tried to see through herself,
and saw instead the eyes of Yuku,
two empty holes
in the sky. Rain listened
to water brushing against reeds

and rushes, the soft
teeth of water clacking on rock,
sky-ladders of water, whole flowers
of rain unfurling, wet toes
and fingers, tongues speaking
the new language of water
on water. Syllables of quenching,
the squelch of mud, thick moisture
in the lungs of red deer running.

Rain fell, and there was no thirst
in the throats of jays and cactus.
Rain cooled feather and spine.

Bobok took off his bat wings,
folding them like a fan, the ribs
gently hushed, wings
like a dried fig.

All the toads sang
as orange poppies exploded with light,
showers of petals flooding the earth.

2

The best way to know God
is through dreams.
I believe in the old ways,
when Yuku and his wide-mouthed
woman dashed rain down,
but there are others who say
when you walk with Dios
he will tell you he's Christian.
So its only fair
that I tell you his version.

Noah, or maybe it was Yaitowi,
heard God's chorus

in his dreams:
Build a boat out of wood,
bind it with tar and rope.
There were a lot of angelic blueprints,
cubits of this, two by two of that.
Yaitowi measured his elbow:
one cubit. Not a Jewish cubit,
but Yaqui, so it had some feathers
and flowers thrown in for good measure.

Then he cut, axed, sawed,
and hammered.

On February 17, 614,
it started to rain.
The sky flooded,
drowning the light.
Everyone climbed
aboard the boat.

The rain fell,
the rain fell, the rain
fell,
the rain.

Those who wanted to be
Christians called Yaitowi "Noah."
Those who wanted to be
themselves
jumped off the boat.
They became animals.
They hear God's voice
in their bellies now.

There were oceans of rain.

On July 17, the waters receded
until on November 1, the Day
of the Dead, land appeared
among drowned bones.

Yaitowi stood
on a hill
with 13 men and 11 women.
Around them, fish gasped,
twisting on the rocks.

On another hill, Emac Dolores
spread her damp hair
across her shoulders.
Later she turned to stone,
only God knows why.
You can see her
near Mount Matuakame.

On every hill, there were a few
alive, faces turned up to the sun.
Even the angels shook their wings.
Domicilia shined her halo
with a bit of her sleeve.
Around her stood 7 birds,
7 donkeys, and 7 dogs.

Perhaps also 7 fleas.

On the 7th day, there was thunder and rain,
not the heaving-breasted wife of Yuku,
not the heavy-stomping Yuku,
not Suawaka and his comets.
Not even the little mud voices of Bobok.
This is the Christian version.

Instead we have dawn breaking like the wings
of angels cracking open heaven.

San Gabriel announced the Voice of God.
The dogs howled, the donkeys kicked up
their heels, and the birds molted in fright.

God said: *I will bless the seraphim
and make men in my image.*

I will put my arch, the rainbow,
over the heavens and altars
so no more will the earth
be destroyed by flood.

As he spoke, it was done.

Then the good men and women asked for glory.
God said: *Drink from the glass*
from which I drink.

And there was no thirst
in the throats of living souls.

There are caves of thieves
and false prophets. There're brothers
who kill and call themselves God.
Do not be deceived.

In the garden of God, which is really Potam village,
green toads listened, spatulate fingers
glistening. *Kawok kawok kawok.*
The reign of god is falling,
the rain the rain the rain.

This was told in the ancient manner,
with much uplifting of palms,
as if testing for rain,
and apparitions of holy women,
circlets of roses around their ankles,
floating on small clouds,
and wise men wandering among
the urgent push of maize seedlings
sprouting from the generations of river-flooded soil;
from village to village the wise voyaged,
sleeping at night under the wings
of swallows folded like prayers.

This happened
as it has been told.
Do not be deceived.

The Red Rose

María lifted the *cántaro*, the water jug made out of red clay, to her shoulder and walked quickly to the river. Her bare, brown feet were dusty but not dirty, since it was the good earth she walked on.

At the edge of the river, her toes slipped in the mud. It felt cool and she smiled. María liked to dip her cántaro into a small whirlpool where the water seemed fresh and lively.

She waded out into the river, her skirt floating on top at first, then soaking up the water and falling slowly into the river like a circle of bright cotton fish around her ankles.

This day, as she lowered the cántaro, she stopped in surprise. A red rose swirled around the whirlpool. She tried to catch it with her hands, but it was spinning too fast. Then she used the cántaro, scooping up the rose in one motion.

María took out the rose and held it close to her face. It was beautiful and smelled sweet. She decided to take it back and show José, her man. She tucked the flower between her breasts, right over her heart, and hurried back.

But when she found José and excitedly told him about the wondrous flower and then reached for it, it was gone! Only the perfume remained.

And this is how Jesus was conceived, from a red flower. From the perfume of a rose and the heart of a woman.

But there is more. Always you should learn what happens behind the story.

At this time, there was God, as always. And he wanted to destroy the people on earth. But the soul of Jesus, the *hiapsi*, talked with God. Jesus said he would make the people better. He would talk to them. God sighed, but agreed.

So God sent Saint Gabriel to all the stars and planets. He announced that there was to be a big meeting. God wanted the universe to agree, also. When the *si'ime buere chokim*, the planets and stars, arrived and heard the matter, they permitted Jesus to be born in a human body.

The angels made the little body. And the stars added good qualities like kindness and love. The planets granted faith and wisdom. The little body grew in the sun's care. It grew into life. The little body became a small baby, a human male. He had no wings. He wasn't an angel. He wasn't a star holding up Earth. He was only a small crying human.

When the stars circled the infant, they saw that his soul was good. The angels chanted. They sang and enchanted.

When Jesus was born, the rooster crowed, "Cristo nació!"

Now you know how he was made and why he came. Now you know why, when you have a good heart, you are closer to God.

And here is something to think about. Jesus was born in a place where the world will come for water. When this happens, the world will end.

Jesus as Hopul Woki (Folded Feet)

Jesus was a Yaqui. He walked from ranchería to ranchería, in the four directions. He wore sandals made out of plant fibers and a straw hat. He crossed the rivers, wading up to his knees in water, and traveled through deserts of thorn bushes and snakes. He was a curer, and possessed *seataka*, a flower body, that is, one full of spirit power. It is a gift given in the womb.

One day, Jesus was walking with San Pedro. It was time to eat, but they had no food. Soon, however, they saw a house, and Jesus sent San Pedro there to get something to eat. When San Pedro returned, he was gnawing on a chicken leg.

"Why does this chicken have only one leg?" Jesus asked his follower.

"Oh," replied San Pedro, "all the chickens in this part of the country have just one leg."

He pointed to a tree in the yard where many chickens were sleeping, standing on one leg, with the other folded up under their feathers.

"Look! Just as I told you," said San Pedro.

Jesus picked up a rock and threw it. When it hit a chicken, the bird squawked, then stood on both feet.

"Oh!" cried San Pedro, "a miracle!"

Then he smiled, and taking up several small stones, he threw them at the flock.

"See," said San Pedro, "I can perform miracles, too!"

They say that the first Spanish priests came carrying a cross, and the Yaquis approved since they already believed in the importance of the four directions.

The cross is referred to as Itom Ae Santísima Cruz, or Our Mother Most Holy Cross, but the cross is not female. It is male and wears a robe with rosary, which is made of rolled and dried rose petals.

When Jesus was killed, his blood became red roses, flowers that fell to the earth. When Jesus died, the angels took off their crowns. When he died, he was nailed to the cross he had made himself, and his feet were folded over.

Radiating in All Directions

The Aztecs came from someplace in northwestern Mexico, maybe close to Yaqui country. According to tradition, the Aztecs emerged from under the earth through seven caves and settled in Aztlán, which was an island of white herons. Aztlán means "Place of Whiteness" and alludes to the heron's plumage.

Then, in the fourteenth century, the Aztecs migrated south, looking for a sign to show them where they should settle again. They were led by a brother and sister, Huitzilopochtli (Left-handed Hummingbird), who represented the sun god, and Malinal Xochitl (Grass Flower), who was the moon.

By this time, the Aztecs and Yaquis (or Yoemem, the People) were certainly distinct tribes, sharing only a common linguistic base, Nahuatl.

Nevertheless, there were connections between the two groups, especially through trading. Although it is almost one thousand miles from Sonora to Mexico City (or Tenochtitlán, as it was called then, the name referring to red prickly pears —and also to the human hearts that were sacrificed to the sun), Indian runners supplied fresh, living fish for the tables of Moctezuma. Their endurance and speed is well noted today, especially among the Tarahumaras. They made the trip in a matter of hours, not days.

Trade routes were well established, radiating in all directions from Tenochtitlán. Messengers took news to the outlying districts, and delegates contributed the necessary tribute or taxes to the city. So events of importance that happened in Tenochtitlán also affected the rest of Mexica. Certainly, the invasion of Cortés sent ripples—no, tidal waves—throughout Mexica, and the resulting changes and sicknesses touched the lives of every single Mexican in every tribe.

The Iron of Their Lances

Vanished glories . . .
nothing recalls them
but the written page.
—*Hungry Coyote (Nezahualcoyotl),*
1401–1472, Texcoco

The following poem is from the words of an anonymous Aztec poet.

A.D. 1519

The iron of their lances
glistened from afar;
the shimmer of their swords
was as of a sinuous watercourse.
Their iron breast
and back pieces, their helmets clanked.
Some came completely cased in iron.
And ahead of them
ran their dogs,
panting,
with foam continually dripping
from their muzzles.

1520

They charged the crowd
with their iron lances and hacked
us with their iron swords.
They slashed the backs of some;
they hacked at the shoulders
of others,
splitting

their bodies
open.

The blood of the young warriors
ran like water;
it gathered in pools.
And the Spaniards began to hunt
them out of the administrative buildings,
dragging out
and killing
anyone
they could find,
even starting to take those buildings
to pieces
as they searched.

1521

At about this time,
when the Spaniards had fled from Mexico,
there came a great sickness,
a pestilence, the smallpox.
It spread over the people
with great destruction. . . .
The brave Mexican warriors
were indeed weakened by it.
It was after all
this had happened
that the Spaniards
came back.

Fighting continued,
both sides took captives,
on both sides there were deaths. . . .
Great became the suffering
of the common folk.
There was hunger.

Many died of famine.
The people ate anything—
lizards
barn swallows
corn leaves
salt grass

The enemy pressed
about us like a wall.
They herded us.
Great was the stench
of the dead
so that we became orphans,
O my sons!
So we became
when we were young.
All of us were thus.
We were born
to die.

Bird Killer

A messenger from the south, from the great city of Tenochtitlán, has told us this day of a terrible and inconceivable thing.

At the time of the last corn planting, when the river floods the fields, strange men entered the city for the second time.

"Wait," said a young woman. "You say the second time . . . ?"

The messenger nodded between gulps of sweet water. He sat down on a deerskin and we all found places around him. He told us about the strangers who came and took control of the palaces and of Moctezuma himself. They became so arrogant that they were forced out of the city, but they returned a year later and strangled the Aztec ruler.

They have killed the children by running them through with long knives and bashing their heads against the stone walls. They have raped the girls and garroted the women. They have cut off the heads of the men. The small boys they throw to their big dogs.

The messenger paused, taking a deep breath. "I've told this to many people. I've traveled for weeks. But I still can't talk easily about it."

We waited while he calmed himself.

"This man—their leader is called Cortés—ordered that all the aviaries in the city be torched."

An old woman asked, puzzled, "He killed the birds?"

The messenger nodded. Cortés set fire to the bamboo cages. The hummingbirds with their iridescent feathers flared into tiny puffs of light. The herons fell in blackened lumps onto the red clay floor. The parrots with their noble feathers of green, blue, turquoise, and yellow were burnt, beaks and bones crushed into the stinking mass.

"These strangers were white like ash and bones. They have killed the voices of the city. They killed our spirit," said the man.

We don't know what this has to do with us. It's good we live so far away. But some of us think that it will affect us, too. When a comet falls in the sky, though it is far from us, we know something bad will happen. Everything is connected. Moctezuma was such a comet.

While we gave the messenger bowls of cooked maize and slices of soft new squash, we sent our own messengers to other towns along the river.

The messenger scooped up the maize with a bone spoon. "I'm going north again," he said, "and I won't return."

Our women tied feathers from wild canaries in his hair while he cried.

We said good-bye, and he never looked back.

Cortés burned the aviaries on June 15, 1521.

The Woman Who Measured Yaqui Country

Her name was Ana María and she was a wise woman, a Sea Hamut. She was asked by the Yaquis to measure the breadth of their lands. She had the knowledge but not the strength, so she hired a giant to help her.

His voice was a mountain. His shoulders were the ramparts of the sea. His legs were rivers of stone. He took one of his arrows, made from the backbone of a whale, and shot it once toward Guaymas.

Then he fitted another arrow made from the black stone, the magnet, and shot it west toward Ba'a poosi. And finally, he shot a last arrow, one made of bird dreams, north to Ta kala'im. With these three arrows, he formed a triangle that delineated Yaqui country.

There were markers at the three points when the Spaniards came.

The Snake People

Habiel Mo'el was a lazy young man. He combed his hair with his fingers and washed his mouth by licking it with his tongue.

His parents were dead, but he had many relatives and he visited them every day, eating their food. He liked fiestas and long talks over bowls of rabbit stew. He slept late in the morning. Waking, he'd blink his eyes, then stumble to the water gourd. Habiel would take a deep drink, then another, the last swishing around in his dry mouth, capturing all of the previous meal's flavors, before swallowing his "morning soup."

He never did much work. And he never stayed with any one relative too long. He lived by himself in a small, rude shack at the foot of the hill Mete'etomakame.

One day he heard about a fiesta that was to be held on the other side of the *monte*. He knew where the road was, but it was far away and he was too lazy. He decided to take a shortcut.

He started out whistling, looking forward to fine food and pretty girls. He swung a stout club in front of him, twirling it and dancing a little. Soon, though, the hot sun plastered his hair to his scalp. He stopped whistling. Dragging the club behind him, he trudged through the woods.

The trees were thick with thorns. He had to crawl on his knees, ducking his head low. The thorns tore at his arms. Burrs stuck in his hair. He crept on his stomach under stiff branches. His skin itched. But worst of all, he was hungry.

Growing more irritable by the second, Habiel emerged from the dense trees. Still on his hands and knees, his head drooping, he caught his breath. Then he stood up, wiping the sweat from his brow.

He hadn't taken one step when a big snake slithered across his path.

"¡Ay!" Habiel struck the snake with his big club. He raised his arm to strike again, but the snake hurried away.

Habiel walked a little farther, over a small rise, and stopped, startled. There before him was a large pueblo. Many people walked about and the smell of food filled the air. He licked his lips.

When he reached the pueblo, a guard approached him.

"The chief wisssshesss to sssee you," he said, so Habiel followed, puzzled at the man's curious way of speaking.

Inside the house, it was dark. Habiel stood a second, letting his eyes adjust. He saw an old man sitting on a bench. Next to him was a young girl, her waist wrapped in leaves.

"Ssstand, Habiel, before usss!"

Habiel shifted nervously on his feet. This was very strange. He had expected a guest's welcome: pots of food, some cool water. But he wasn't invited to sit. And strangest of all, they knew his name. Perhaps, he thought, they're some distant relatives who had heard of his handsome looks.

The old man glared at him. "Why did you hit thisss girl?"

Habiel was stunned. "I never hit any girl!"

"Don't lie! On your way through the desssert, you hit her. She'sss quite hurt, can't you sssee?"

The slender girl pulled away a corner of the leaf bandage. Habiel could see a large bruise.

"I swear it wasn't me. I didn't hit her!"

She looked at him. "But it wasss you, and look, there'sss hisss heavy club. That'sss what he hit me with!"

Habiel shook his head. "No, it wasn't me."

"You almossst killed me," she hissed. "You would have, I think, if I hadn't got away."

Habiel felt the hairs on the back of his neck rise. Something was very wrong here. He looked closer at the girl. Her eyes had no white in them. Her face was broad across the eyes, tapering down by the chin. He was frightened and begged their pardon.

The old man whispered with the girl. She nodded. The chief stood up.

"You may go. Sssince thisss isss your firssst offenssse and you've asssked our pardon, you may leave. But never hit anyone again."

Habiel backed out of the house quickly. When he turned around, the pueblo was gone. He spun back to the house. It, too, had disappeared.

But in the dirt he saw many curving tracks, the trails of snakes, and in the sound of the wind he heard their voices: sssssssss.

A Line on the Earth

When Captain Diego de Guzmán arrived at the Río Yaqui, he saw the fields of maize, beans, cotton, tobacco, and squash as an extension of Spain. He proclaimed all the inhabitants subjects of the king and queen of Spain. He renamed the river, the *hiak vatwe*, calling it the Río San Francisco. It no longer owed its allegiance to the rains in the mountains and the long fertile valley that stretched to the sea, which Guzmán also renamed.

All of the reeds and fish and animals were given new names. Naming is possession. He possessed in the names of the king and queen. Yet under the new sounds covering the delicate edges of leaves and the curling fins of white-flashing *kuchu* (fish), all remained the same. The *aiya* was still the tree near where the water went down, *vatakomsikapo*. The red ant was still the *eeye*.

The Yoemem stood at the edges of their villages. They saw strangers with hair covering their chins. They saw sunburnt faces with strips of peeling skin and the soulless gaze of white-rimmed eyes.

The Spaniards kept a journal, along with maps, ink, and quills, all rolled up in leather tubes and tied around the waist of the most literate. On October 4, 1533, a Spaniard wrote that many warriors waited for them in a large field. As the Spaniards advanced, the Yaquis threw fistfuls of dirt into the air and yelled, shaking their bows. The Yaqui leader was an old man who was clothed in a black robe studded with pearls. He carried a wooden staff with a fancy handle and was surrounded by dogs, birds, and deer. When the sunlight fell on him, he gleamed with silver.

The old man took his staff and drew a line on the earth. If the Spaniards crossed that line, it would be death. No words were spoken, but the Spaniards understood. Captain Guzmán recorded that he then offered food in a placating tone of voice.

The Yoemem, the Yaquis, countered the offer: all would be well if the strangers allowed themselves to be tied up.

The Spaniard then wrote that the soldiers aimed their heaviest cannon at them and fired as they shouted "Santiago!"

The battle didn't last long. The Spaniards retreated, claiming themselves the victors. They were masters at naming something other than it was.

The Spanish chronicler, however, did note that the Yaquis were excellent fighters. Because the field was so flat, it offered few strategic opportunities other than for straight hand-to-hand combat. Otherwise, admitted the Spaniard, the Yaquis would have inflicted more damage. Out of seventeen horses, twelve were wounded and one killed.

Later that night, an old Yaqui man slipped into Guzmán's camp and offered him a gift: three maces encrusted with chunks of fine turquoise. Instead of noting the ceremonial beauty of the war clubs — for it was unlikely that they were functional — the Spaniards were struck only with the possibility of further wealth.

Although the Spaniards were forced to return to their garrison in the south, they resolved to return at a later date for slaves and other riches.

Head of a Cow and Other White Men from Heaven

In 1527, Álvar Núñez Cabeza de Vaca lost his way on the Florida coast. He and three other companions wandered through swamps, deserts, badlands, and mirages. They crossed the vast lands now called Texas and the Mexican state of Chihuahua. They climbed mountains and descended just north of the Río Yaqui, where they turned south, heading toward the Spanish settlement at Culiacán.

At one point, earlier in their journey, they had been imprisoned by Indians, but by the time they reached the Sonoran desert in 1536, they were revered as healers. Throngs of Indians from many tribes accompanied them.

The Río Yaqui starts in the Sierra Madre, then winds its way down and westward into the heart of the Opata homelands before it meets the sea. Cabeza de Vaca saw an Opata wearing a sword buckle. It had a little horseshoe nail sewn into it. The Opatas said that the white men had come from heaven. They described animals that had to be horses and pointed south, where more white men lived.

The Spaniards followed the river until they came to Yaqui country and saw the fields with their carefully tended crops. They saw the plump pods of beans and the long-leafed maize. The Yaquis gave Cabeza de Vaca and his entourage more than two thousand baskets of maize. He continued south toward Culiacán, this man with the strange name: head of a cow, Cabeza de Vaca. The closer he got to the Spanish settlement, the more he saw how the land had been ravaged. Villages were abandoned. Starvation and slavery had wiped out most of the inhabitants. The survivors had fled.

When he reached his fellow countrymen, he told them stories of mountains made of gold. These tales inspired more Spaniards to invade the northern territory.

Note: Cabeza de Vaca supposedly received his surname from an ancestor who helped guide a king by placing the skull of a cow on the correct road somewhere in Spain.

Throwing Fire at the Sun

> This day we saw ten or twelve Indians on shore.
> —*from the log book of Francisco de Ulloa*

"Someone with one big eye is looking at us," whispered Sewa, an old woman. She stood on the beach, holding her grandson's hand. Nearby, several other Yoemem waited, watching the small ship creak its slow way past the long beaches.

They were a small people, with bright feathers around their wrists and fastened to their hair. Sewa had blue tattoos on her chin and cheeks, thin blue lines that looked like the edge of sky where it meets the sea. Her ears were pierced; small pink shells dangled from them. Her daughter had pierced her nose, but that wasn't to Sewa's liking. They were an independent people, strongly individualistic but united as a people when war with neighboring tribes threatened. She tugged at her woven grass skirt and squatted down on the sand. Her grandson plopped down next to her.

"What is it?" He pointed to the ship. The sails hung limply from the mast.

"It's not a giant tree with white butterfly wings."

He nodded and waited. He now knew it wasn't that, but what was it? He knew what a boat was. His people made small boats from bound reeds. Sometimes they fished the big water, *kalifornia vaawe*, but they were not a sea people like the Kunkaak, who caught huge fish and knew how to sing like the sea. His people, the Yoemem, tended the fields and hunted in the mountains.

His small, rough fingers traced the hard muscles in his grandmother's arms. She sat thinking, squinting at the strange boat. Her long dark hair brushed against his cheek, and he leaned into her comforting presence.

"They are looking at us," she told him. She knew they were hairy men, the same foul-smelling devils who had tried to steal some of the Yoemem a few years earlier. There had been a battle and her people had won, but the air above the villages had been tainted for days.

"Who is looking at us?" Her grandson was persistent. "Why do they have only one eye?"

She put her arm around him. "When they're not looking at us, they have two eyes. When they look at us, they bring out another eye that they keep in a long stick."

He shivered. "Are they monsters?"

She lifted her chin. "They're not Yoemem."

Ah, he said to himself. This explained everything. What was not from the Yoemem, the People, was not to be understood in human terms.

Sewa gazed at the ship. Her necklace, her *kookam*, fashioned from pearls and strung iridescent shells, quivered between her naked breasts. Was it her heart trembling in fear or anger? Or was it the kookam itself shaking, remembering the swelling sea, rising and falling like Sewa's breath?

Around her more Yoemem were muttering quietly. The men's fists were clenched. They hadn't forgotten the last battle. Sewa remembered how her cousin had looked the day he faced the white men. Wearing a headdress made of dark red cotton cloth and decorated with pearly shells from the sea, he stood nervously adjusting the coyote skin that hung down from the back of the headdress nearly to his hips. Owl feathers were sewn in three places on the headdress. He carried his bow, *kuta wiko'i*, made of *kungwo* wood. Testing the deer sinew bowstring, he had nodded, satisfied. Then he checked the arrows in the rawhide quiver, *hu'itoria*, that he had decorated with bits of hammered silver. The arrows were made of fire-hardened bamboo cane and fletched with more owl feathers. Finally he had been ready, and Sewa thought how handsome he'd looked, a warrior of skill and spirit.

> Because of the distance, we could not see what sort of people
> they were, but they seemed to be naked.
> —*from the log book*

Sewa got up smoothly. She was still a strong woman. Her grandson followed her back to the house. It was time to sleep a little. The sun was hot.

> [They] make no sacrifices, nor have idols, but they
> worship the sun like heathens.
> —*anonymous Spaniard*

Five people decided to stay on the beach while the others returned to their sleeping mats.

Under the cool willow roofs, they closed their eyes, wondering about men who wore heavy bright hats in the heat of the day. Men who covered their faces like animals with fur. Who rode big dogs with hooves like a deer. Who said the world was theirs, even the sea and the air.

Sewa's brother had a dream. When he woke, he told his family that the sun was dying. "Mu kuk uta." The sun was dying, like a burned flower. The wind stopped, the maize withered, the sea was still.

"Quickly, I threw fire at the sun!" In his dream, he threw fire and the fire consumed his fingers, then his hands. It swallowed his torso, the way a red fish swallows a twisting larva.

"Then the sun came back," he continued, spreading his fingers in the air. "But I was only a shadow, a soul with no center." He cried while his family stroked his gray hair.

Dreams were respected. Sometimes what happened in a dream was obviously related directly to waking life. This dream was not so easy to understand. Everyone knew the sun died for a short time. It happened rarely, but it was not unusual, and then the people scooped up fire in hollowed gourds and threw it at the sun.

And sometimes the moon died and you had to throw water at it or place little flat shells of water around your house. Then you could see the moon again, shining all around you, its wavery light, pale and luminous.

It was well known that when the moon died, many women would also die that year. That was the way it was. Always.

The moon, Mala Mecha, mother moon. We came from the moon and it is the mother of all women. Yes, the moon. The sea. The women. This was one force of life.

And when the sun died, many men would die.

"Perhaps," suggested one of the brother's sisters, "your dream is the opposite." She said this hopefully, pursing her lips. "Maybe the sun will not die. Maybe no one will die."

"Don't go hunting tomorrow," advised a visiting cousin. If a man hunted when the sun died, he would die.

The sun. The hunt. The men. That was another force of life.

Sewa raised herself up from her sleeping mat and leaned on one elbow. "I think it's about changes. It is about those hairy men."

A woman nodded, then sipped water from the drinking gourd, shook the last drop free, and hung the gourd back on the fire post in the center of the house. "It is about our world turning black. It is about us becoming only shadows with no bright centers."

At the end of the discussion, no one knew what the dream meant, but the accumulation of theories gave them all something to think about. The more you knew about a thing, the better you could understand it. Or at least learn how to react to it.

Which was why the Yoemem kept a careful watch on the ship and the hairy men.

> At night, they made us two or three signal fires on the coast.
> —*from the log book*

The *chokim*, the stars, were the souls of those who had died. There were many in the sky, watching the ship anchored offshore.

Sewa pulled a cotton blanket around her shoulders. She sat with the fire at her back so that she could view the stars, and she wondered which star was her mother.

The waves rolled in, a steady sound, and the fires hissed and crackled. Now and then someone spoke, a voice murmuring, and all the sounds were the way the night waits. The sand was still warm from the heat of the day, but the air was cooling. The ship rose and fell with the gentle swell of the sea; stars clustered around it.

Sewa's granddaughter talked to another young woman on the other side of the fire. Their heads were close together and they whispered behind their hands. In spite of the worrisome ship, her granddaughter's eyes were bright with amusement. Perhaps they spoke of young men and flowers left in doorways.

Sewa's name meant flower. Most girls received a flower name. In a land of desert, dependent on rain and river, flowers were considered especially beautiful. But there was a spiritual aspect to flowers: they were beauty and life. They were the blossoms that became the nourishment. The showy, petaled, yellow squash blossom became the full-bellied gourd. Flowers nourished the soul, food the body. In the other world, the spirit world, there were flowers everywhere, even in the sky. Sewa thought that at certain times she could feel the petals brushing her cheeks and she knew she was old. That year even the stars seemed closer. She looked up at the night sky and there at the edge of the light cast by the fires she saw the Milky Ashes.

She turned around, tucking the ends of the blanket under her feet. A young man who had fought against the hairy men several years earlier leaned forward, elbows perched on his knees.

"Perhaps the *yorim*, those hairy strangers, will see our fires and think they're stars. Maybe they'll think we're star souls and that Father Sun, Achai Ta-Ah, has taken away all life. Yes, we're all dead. So they'll leave us."

His friend kicked a rock into the fire and snorted. "You're dreaming. Have you forgotten how we fought those yorim? We're men, not stars. We can fight them and kill them and their dogs."

"Something about the yorim makes my dreams turn inside out." There was a silence, then he continued. "They talk about good things, a great father spirit, but they do evil things. They made loud noises from that big stick and the air was stinking. And they don't look whole and strong. They have souls that stink, too."

"We can still kill them." His friend stabbed a stick into the sand. "They won't leave us unless we kill them.

"Or until we're all dead." He stood up and walked away into the darkness.

An old man poked at the fire, adding another piece of driftwood. He remembered his days of fighting the Mayos. He never liked to listen to talk, he wanted only action. Yet it was the way of the Yoemem to discuss issues. Because there was no one leader during times of peace and no ruling class to dictate how everyone should think, there was always lots of talk. They talked about everything, making up their minds individually. Ideas were valued. Material goods—a hoe, a weapon, clothing of hides or cloth, woven mats—were of less concern. It was the mind and the spirit that interested the Yoemem. Unless you were a young man. Then your body urged you to run, to fight, to love, to be full of life.

Aloud, he wondered if everything was changing. Was it still the way of his youth?

The young warrior took his time answering. "Everything has already changed. Those hairy men have new weapons. Did you hear them? Like thunder breaking mountains!" He snapped a branch and threw it into the fire. "We're good fighters. We can win battles, but at what cost? And for how long? Those yorim like death. And you have heard how they take men and women. I'm not afraid of dying and I won't be a slave. I don't understand what is happening, but I do know that I will fight. I *will* kill them."

His friend's voice floated out of the night. "And when you're dead, your child won't have a father and your wife will be alone. Then the hairy men will take them. We can't fight their evil."

The young warrior stood up. "Be quiet! I *will* fight! If you're afraid, run away to the mountains. Run away to the Mayos!"

A stick flew out of the darkness and struck the warrior in the chest. It fell harmlessly onto the sand. He slowly turned his back and crossed his arms, daring his friend to come out of the night and hit him again. It was an insult. Sewa heard a gasp in the darkness, then the sound of feet running away.

The warrior's shoulders relaxed and he looked over his shoulder. "You see, those hairy men turn us against ourselves. We must kill them."

He left, striding in the same direction as his friend.

There was a deep silence after his departure. The fire burned slowly, the salt in the driftwood sending up sparks of many colors, the smoke twisting up toward the stars. Sewa felt the bones in her body begin to dissolve into filaments of light.

Columbus Dies in Two Ways and It's Still Not Enough to Change History

1540

When Yomumuli left the Surem, some of them ran away from the pueblos into the mountains. In those days, they were small and fat. They couldn't run very fast on their stubby legs. If they got going too fast, arms pumping, cheeks puffing, they'd trip and tumble, tumble, until they rolled to a stop. Rubbing the knots on their heads or shins, they'd chuckle and slap their knees.

One day they were watching the Surem-who-became-Yaquis eating some deer meat from a pot. When the Yaquis went back down the mountain to their homes in the valley, the Surem hurried to the campsite. The fire was cold, the logs charred. They stared at it for a long time.

Then one of the Surem ran back to his hole in the mountain. When he returned he was carrying a pot he'd stolen a while ago.

Smiling, he placed it on top of the dead fire.

All the Surem stood around watching the pot on the dead fire.

They watched it for a long time.

Suddenly one of them smacked himself on the side of the head the way he'd seen Yaquis do sometimes. Only, this Surem knocked himself over. When he sat up, he grinned and pulled himself to his feet. He swayed clumsily up the trail.

Soon he returned with a dead rabbit.

He threw it in the pot.

They all watched the dead rabbit in the pot on the dead fire.

They watched it for a long time.

Then one of them nodded. He started the others nodding. They stood in a circle and nodded. Then he reached in the pot and pulled off a chunk of rabbit, raw meat and fur, and ate it.

The Surem laughed and patted him on the back. Soon all of them were eating the raw meat.

Now, they thought, *we are just like real Yaquis*.

It was not until many years later that they learned to make a fire and cook the meat.

Maybe the Surem, the little people, are a bit stupid. Maybe not. After all, they left the pueblos and the destiny of the Yaquis because they were afraid they couldn't handle such terrible changes. So maybe they were wise enough to know their true nature.

Before Yomumuli left, she put several chiefs in charge of the remaining people. One of them was Omteme. His name meant "He Is Angry." He governed from a mountaintop.

One day he saw Columbus sailing into Guaymas. This made Omteme mad, because he knew the prophecies. He knew Columbus was up to no good. The talking stick had told everyone this.

Columbus climbed a big hill and saw Omteme in the distance stomping his feet. Omteme yelled, "What do you want from us?"

Columbus took a big gun and shot at Omteme. The ball exploded at the bottom of Omteme's mountain.

"I said, what do you want from us?" Omteme didn't understand about guns. He heard only a loud noise that meant nothing to him. He thought it was how the Spaniards talked. Noise but no meaning.

Columbus took aim and fired again. This time the shot was a little bit closer. Omteme shook his fist. "Hey, what do you want from us?"

When Columbus shot the third time, the ground exploded close to Omteme.

"So you want war, eh?" Omteme shouted. He took his bow and, fitting the arrow to the string, pulled back with all his strength. The arrow flew in a high arc that dropped straight to the hill Columbus was standing on. The impact split the hill in two, and Columbus fell into the sea, where he drowned.

"That's it," declared Omteme to his people. "I'm not staying here any longer. Come with me if you want." Then he went into the heart of his mountain.

Many of the people went with him.

Those of us who remained are still asking, "What do you want of us?"

Amongʃt the Moʃt Barbarouʃ and Fierce Peopleʃ

Father Andrés Pérez de Ribas was born in Córdoba, Spain. In 1603, when he was twenty-seven years old, he was sent as a priest to New Spain. He remained near Mexico City while he prepared for his ministry in the northwestern frontier. In 1604, he set out with Captain General Diego Martínez de Hurdaide. While he journeyed and served in Sinaloa and Sonora, he kept a journal, which has been published in English translation as *History of the Triumphs of Our Holy Faith amongʃt the Moʃt Barbarouʃ and Fierce Peopleʃ of the New World*.

For sixteen years, the Jesuit met with the Mayos and Yaquis. He wrote down their practices and customs as he understood them. From our modern viewpoint, he is not the unbiased scholar, but then he never pretended to be. He was a Spaniard, from a distinguished family, and a Jesuit historian. Each of these three elements accounts for his careful prose, his detailed descriptions, and his fervor for the fire that burns in the hearts of the Company of Jesus. Although his religious convictions differ from mine, I can understand (as a scholar myself) his excitement for spiritual conquest in the context of the times. He wrote that the Yaquis were savage and uncultured. He lamented the huge task before him, that of converting a pagan people, but he was pleased that God had given this glorious task to the "Catholic Spaniard of the civilized world." These words, *savage, fierce, uncultured*, of course grate on my nerves as a modern Yaqui. Nevertheless, Pérez de Ribas's journal is the only account we have of Yaqui ways now lost to acculturation. For that reason, I respect his skills of observation and writing.

In this book I quote Father Pérez de Ribas many times. The poem "Ceremony of Adoption of Orphaned Children" relies on information he recorded. As most modern students know, diseases imported from Europe killed native people indiscriminately and ferociously. It's been estimated that 90 percent of native populations were wiped out by disease—only 10 percent survived. Smallpox, measles, tuberculosis, cholera destroyed families, clans, villages, tribes, nations.

This poem may also be about the "adoption" of young boys into tribal male societies. New translations of Pérez de Ribas continue to offer insights into this ceremony. As you'll see in the poem, sandpaintings similar to those still made during some Native American ceremonies in the southwestern United States were part of the Yaqui and Mayo ceremony for orphans. Colored sand and crushed rocks and minerals were poured into tubes of cane that were stopped with a finger at one end. Careful release of the finger allowed the sand to trickle out into desired lines and shapes.

Pérez de Ribas wrote, "They painted mainly two figures that appeared to be human; one they called Variseva. The other was called Vairubi, who was said to be the mother of the first figure. They spoke with much confusion about what these figures represented, like the blind who lack divine light. It even seemed that they spoke of them with a glimpse of God and His Mother, for they referred to them as the first beings, from whom the rest of mankind was born. Nevertheless, everything they said was confusing."

Well, it was probably not so much "confusion" as a disinclination on the part of the Indian men to talk to outsiders, the *padres*, about something so holy. If there really was confusion, it is my guess that the rituals and figures were so ancient that time had unraveled some of their meaning.

It must be remembered that not only time but also migrations had distanced the people from their origins. (See the poem "We Came This Way.") Recently, I found a book that shows ancient cave paintings from Baja California, which is across the Gulf of California from Yaqui country. In Baja, there are many caves that have been painted with natural pigments. These drawings are similar in style to the paintings of Neolithic cave artists in Europe, yet they retain some exciting differences. The animals, of course, are those indigenous to the area: rattlesnakes, rabbits, deer, whales, manta rays. The people are drawn with red and black pigments, some half and half. The women's breasts are drawn from a side view even though the rest of the body is frontal. Strange rayed creatures sit on their shoulders. Men shoot arrows at other men or animals. The drawings are hauntingly beautiful and mysterious. Even the local Indians don't know who drew them: it is such a long time ago. Their ancestors have come and gone, in memory as well as time.

In Yaqui country, the Jesuits were faced with a more contemporary art: the sandpaintings that represented ancient ceremonies vital to the tribe. After forbidding the Yaquis to draw Vairubi, they encouraged more Catholic images. Yet they still felt that the spirit of the drawings was not truly Catholic and introduced other activities to substitute for the ceremonies. They taught the Indians to enter the church dancing and to pray to God and the Virgin for protection of their crops.

In "A Cloud of Arrows," I quote Pérez de Ribas's description of a battle between the Yaquis and Hurdaide. Eight thousand Yaqui warriors battled for a day and a night, almost capturing the captain general. It was the custom then for victors to cut off the heads of their vanquished enemies and display them at victory dances. Often, warriors used poisoned arrows. One arrow, not poisoned, pierced the steel visor of Hurdaide's helmet. We can imagine the strength of the warrior who launched that arrow and the skill that went into making it. The Yaquis also used psychology in warfare. While the Spaniards roasted in their metal armor, the Yaquis rested conspicuously in the shade, drinking cool water the women brought in clay jars. The Spaniards were reduced to sucking dryly on musket balls.

Pérez de Ribas tells how, during the battle, Yaquis stole the Spaniards' gunpowder, started a fire in order to force the Europeans down from their hilltop advantage, and looted the Spaniards' baggage. Only a trick involving stampeding horses enabled the Spanish force to get away. The rest of the account goes on to tell about an unnamed woman leader and emissary who traveled the no-man's-land between the Mayos and Yaquis in order to reach the Jesuits and the soldiers. The Yaquis wanted peace. They also wanted the support of the Spaniards against their enemies, especially the Mayos, a tribe living south of Yaqui territory.

"Oh, My Grandfather" is an entire quotation from Pérez de Ribas. I find the attitude he conveys offensive, but his description of the old ways is interesting. He says the Yaquis called the devil "Grandfather," but since this is a term of respect, the term probably meant "ancient one," or someone old enough to have wisdom. Because Pérez de Ribas viewed everything from the perspective of Jesus versus the devil, he could not often see past his own spiritual and intellectual limitations. He does give a clear picture of the oral tradition at work—the speaker in the center of the village, the tobacco pipes in the hands of the listeners, the words booming around the plaza. This is so universally "Indian" that a Mohawk from northeastern North America would have felt right at home in the scene. Pérez de Ribas also lets us see that the individual's opinion was important to the consensus of the whole. This, too, is a very Indian concept, in direct contrast to the European way of thinking, with its feudal hierarchies and lack of individual rights.

I was particularly excited about reading Pérez de Ribas's chapter "Origin of

These People and Their Diversity of Languages." The padre theorized that "these people arrived from Asia overland to the north or crossed some narrow stretch of sea that was easy to cross and remains as yet undiscovered." He questioned the oldest people, who all said they had come from the north, where other tribes had taken their territory. I wrote a poem, "We Came This Way," about this. I note at the end of the poem that it wasn't for another 150 years that Bering "discovered" the strait named after him. This strait is a narrow sea between Asia and Alaska. The oral tradition of the people in Sonora and Sinaloa was an accurate memory. There is also another memory among Yaquis, that we came from the area of the Pima and Colorado Rivers, north of the border. The direction of the migrations are always north to south.

Pérez de Ribas talks about the similarities between the root words of the Yaquis and the Aztecs. He tells us that many languages (dialects) were spoken within a tribe. Of course, language was important to him for evangelical purposes. He admits that to preach to the people in their own language is very powerful.

In his journal, he gives other descriptions that I've used in this book, such as how the women were dressed. Yaquis dyed their skin orange, using wild mulberry juice. Indigo was used to color loops of cotton that were hung on their ears. The loops were decorated with shells and bright rocks. Nose piercing was common, "from the center cartilage." Women wore little in the way of clothing, often going topless. Men usually went naked. Some chiefs wore the skins of jaguars. Rabbit fur was also used, as well as deerskin. Mescal plants and cotton were woven.

Men acquired their names through warfare. After a battle, when the enemies' heads were displayed, drums would beat and the warriors would get drunk. Even after the Jesuits made many changes in Yaqui culture, they could not get the men to use Christian surnames; they preferred their war names.

In one section of his book, Pérez de Ribas commented that what he had written was the exact truth. Can truth be exact? Even Pérez de Ribas acknowledged that his history was inconclusive, but whereas he said that this was because history was still unfolding, I say that it is because he could not think like a Yaqui. Pérez de Ribas's truth is just that: Pérez de Ribas's truth, based on his life as a Catholic Spaniard. It is not the whole truth, the exact truth, or the unbiased truth.

And yet, I much prefer his writing to that of Father Och, who wrote about his experiences in Sonora in a book called *Missionary in Sonora: Travel Reports of Joseph Och, S.J., 1755–1767*. Father Och wrote with a sneered lip. I used his words and persona for the poem "Indian Vices." He believed that Indians were "very lazy and sworn enemies of work." He said that Indians would rather starve than farm. Yaquis were (and still are) the best farmers of northwestern Mexico. With Och's attitude, it's easy to see why Indians would rather have starved than work for him.

Much of the other material in the rest of Part One comes from my reading of *Cycles of Conquest*, by Edward Spicer. He gave me the gist of historical facts on battles and negotiations between Yaquis and the Mexican government in the eighteenth and nineteenth centuries. I also gleaned insights from reading Evelyn Hu-DeHart's research on Yaqui society and culture. She kindly sent me a photocopy of her work.

The reader will, I hope, make the connection between General Torres's regulations (see "Another Trail of Tears") and those of Nazi Germany and its treatment of its "undesirables."

The start of the twentieth century singled out Yaquis for particular cruelties and humiliations. Children were sold, people transported the breadth of Mexico, families murdered. My grandparents left Mexico forever in the early 1900s, traveling up to Arizona and California. Their stories are told in Part Two, "Cuentos de Mi Familia / Stories of My Family."

Vairuba and the Snake

Two weeks after the messenger left, Vairuba dropped her hoe in the maize fields and went home. She had a terrible headache. Her skin felt as if it were crawling with little ants. She scratched and shivered.

Inside her house, she curled up on the sleeping mat and pulled a rabbit fur blanket over her body. Her grandmother startled her by moaning. In the dim interior, she hadn't realized anyone was here.

"I'm sick, Grandmother," Vairuba explained. "Are you all right?"

"Sick."

A fit of shivering overtook the young Vairuba. Her face was covered with a sudden sweat. The fever rose until she forgot her grandmother's silence. She never noticed her husband crawling to his sleeping mat and huddling under the blanket. He was cold and tried to stir up the fire in the center of the house, but he was too weak and fell back, the dry wood still in his hands.

All night, Vairuba was sick. She vomited on her hair and shoulders. The night was moonless and dark. A fetid smell rose from the ground and swirled like fog above the river.

Vairuba could smell it everywhere. It was coming from her and all the people who lay sick in their houses along the river. It was a smell like a long snake turned inside out, so that the stomach revealed the rotted remains of mice, rats, and dying people. She knew the snake was crawling toward her and she flailed at the night, moaning, listening to the snake's hissing.

In the morning, she was covered with red sores that oozed pus. When she scratched, the pus spurted out, smearing the foulness across her body. She wanted to shed her skin like a snake. It itched and bled.

Soon, sores filled her mouth and the insides of her eyelids. Pus ran into her eyes when she rubbed them. Fluid drained from her ears and matted in her hair until she was stuck to the fiber mat. Inside of her, she felt her baby convulse and die.

The fever came back. She saw her husband rise to fix the fire, but then he floated up out of the smoke hole. She tried to call him back but her tongue was thick with bloody sores.

Her grandmother walked out the door, which had changed into the mouth of the snake.

Vairuba could see all of this although her eyes were matted shut. She was blind.

The feathers she had woven into her hair were yellow and green. She watched them transform into large bright birds with orange beaks. They flew away, taking her baby's soul with them. The soul looked like a ball of feathers with wise eyes.

The snake came closer, rattling her skirt of skulls and hands. The snake hissed into Vairuba's shallow breathing and the rattling distracted Vairuba for a moment. When the moment was gone, so was Vairuba.

Ceremony of Adoption of Orphaned Children

NORTHWESTERN MEXICO,
AROUND 1600

First, two canopies of wood and bamboo
were built. The orphans were escorted there
and given *atole* and honey.[1]
For eight days they remained.

Under the second canopy, the men danced
around a circle of colored sand.
Then they drew figures
by filling small tubes of cane
with tinted sand,
unstopping one end with a finger
to let the sand out.
They drew the Mother Vairubi
and Variseva in wavering lines
of blue and ground pearls.
They drew ears of corn,
beans, and pumpkins.
Serpents,
birds,
ants.
Each morning for eight mornings
they sang and danced.

Then on the ninth day, still singing,
they went to the orphans
and placed their fingers on the children's eyes,
opening them. This was for protection.
The orphans were taken to the sandpaintings
and rubbed all over with birds
and small animals of colored sand.
After this they ate and received gifts
from their foster parents.

When they bathed in the river,
they were a happy family.

Later the priests came,
forbidding the pagan aspect
of sand animals,
so the men drew the Holy Mother
and Child in brown, red, white, yellow, black.
However, because it seemed that this ceremony
touched too closely upon their former celebrations,
the priests wished to remove it from their memory.
Therefore, they ordered that one day during Christmastide
(having abandoned those figures) the Indians should enter
the church dancing and asking God and the Virgin
(whose image was there with her Son in her arms)
for the same things they had formerly sought
through their worthless superstitions.
They were thus instructed and content.

Note: The passage in italics is from the journal of Father Andrés Pérez de Ribas, one of the first Jesuit priests to serve in the Yaqui area. The rest of the poem is based on information included in his journal, "Historia de los triumfos de nuestra santa fee entre gentes las más barbaras y fieras del nuevo Orbe" (1617). The most recent translation—by Daniel Reff, Maureen Ahern, and Richard Danford—includes new insights and some different interpretations. Reff thinks the "orphans" were actually young boys being "adopted" by members of different tribal societies. The children spent a brief time with their adopted families. It was more symbolic than actual, although the boys came to spend more time with their sponsors than with their biological parents. The ceremony was, Reff believes, a rite of passage.

Women were excluded from these ceremonies, such as the one mentioned by Pérez de Ribas in which the "orphans" were taught to "open their eyes." Pérez de Ribas said that some Indians possessed such sight and skill in deflecting enemy arrows that before an arrow could hit or wound them, they turned it from its path with their own bow so that it did not reach its mark. They also gave weapons to the adopted children, and then each one chose a youngster to take home to raise as his own son. Later, Pérez de Ribas recalled this ceremony as he was writing his journal and noted that he thanked God that the Indians no longer remembered this celebration.

The People Are Kind

Francisco de Ibarra was the nephew of a Basque prospector, Diego de Ibarra. He became the governor of a part of northwestern Mexico known previously as Nuevo Galicia but renamed after a Basque province: Nueva Vizcaya. Looking for more silver mines, he turned toward the Río Yaqui.

A member of the expedition, Balthasar de Obregón, kept a record of their encounters with the Yaquis. He described their welcome. Five hundred Yaquis greeted the Europeans with baskets full of fish, game, and foods harvested from fields of maize, squash, and beans.

The Yaquis were dressed colorfully with bright feathers, beads, and seashells. The women wore their hair loose to the waist and were bare breasted. Their skirts were made of green grass. The men carried weapons but wore little clothing, since the climate was mild.

From their discussions, the Spaniards learned that about fifteen thousand men lived in the area from the sea to the mountains. The Europeans were impressed with a large forest that grew nearby and with the river, which was abundant with fish. They also found pearls in the sea and clusters of red coral.

Obregón conceded that the people were very kind in their offers of hospitality.

A Cloud of Arrows

The Yaqui leader Anabaletei, or Ania-bailutek, refused to allow the Spaniard Hurdaide into Yaqui territory. Hurdaide was pursuing two Ocoroni Indians, Lautaro and Babilomo. The Yaquis wouldn't hand them over to Hurdaide. When a delegation of Christianized Indians was sent to parley, Ania-bailutek had them killed. Two were Yaqui women who had been captured years before and converted to Christianity.

Hurdaide returned with a force of two thousand, all Indians from neighboring tribes. Forty Spanish soldiers accompanied the army. They were defeated.

So Hurdaide assembled another army, this time of four thousand Indian foot soldiers and fifty mounted Spaniards. After a battle that lasted one day and one night, he was wounded. The Yaquis, with seven thousand men, almost captured him, but the Spaniards and their forces retreated.

In his report, *History of the Triumphs of Our Holy Faith amongst the Most Barbarous and Fierce Peoples of the New World*, Father Pérez de Ribas wrote that messengers were sent to the Yaqui camp with demands for peace, but that

> the Yaqui nation was so arrogant and haughty that they refused to listen to any discussion of peace. Indeed, they took the captain's message and tied it to a string, and then an Indian dragged it along behind him, making a mockery of it right before the Spaniards' eyes.
>
> All that day and the following night the Yaqui encouraged their people to fight. . . . At the break of dawn all the Yaqui from those eighty rancherías or villages . . . had assembled. They attacked our army as one, with such a great thrust of bows and arrows and screaming that our camp was in great danger. The combat lasted for some time, and many people from both sides were wounded and some were killed. The Yaqui persisted in their anger and fury, having the river in their favor, for it was swollen and the waters had risen. They easily passed from one bank to the other, depending on what best suited their offense or defense. The Spaniards' position was not favorable for combat using their armored horses, and the allied Indians began to lose heart. All this forced the captain to give the order to break camp and retreat.

Captain Hurdaide ordered a retreat through a forest. The Yaq
many trees, which prevented the Spaniards from charging
addition, the felled trees provided protection for the Yaqu

The Indian allies deserted the Spanish army. The
stripped of their heavy armor so that the soldiers coulu
Hurdaide remained behind with twenty-two soldiers and an Inc
refused to retreat with the rest of his warriors.

"The enemy attack on the abandoned captain and his twenty-two soldie.
many of them wounded," commented Father Pérez de Ribas. "The captain himself
[suffered] five arrow wounds to his face and hands. Later I heard him reflecting
upon the hardness of the Indian arrow points, which were made from fire-hardened
wood, as well as the bravery with which they used this weapon. He said that one
of the wounds he had suffered to his face was from the point of an arrow that had
been shot with such force that it penetrated the visor of his helmet, which was made
of collared chain mail."

The captain rallied his soldiers with "great spirit and friendly words" and then
took stock of their ammunition. The Yaquis had captured all their gunpowder,
leaving the Spaniards with only the powder they carried individually in canisters.
The captain and his small force managed to retreat to a small hill. "They were one
and a half leagues from the river and it was already well into the morning when, dur-
ing the summer, the very hot sun beats down on this land," wrote Pérez de Ribas.
"Nevertheless [they] encouraged one another to fight and defend themselves from
the seven thousand warriors surrounding them . . . [who rained] arrows down on
the captain and his men."

Then the Yaqui attempted another battle strategy. When they saw that the place
to which the Spaniards had retreated was full of weeds and was like a dry field
of straw . . . they set fire to the field. . . . As soon as they started the fire with the
little sticks that they use in place of flint, tinder, and steel, the captain, who was
very skillful in undoing these nations' stratagems, ordered for fire to be taken
from the flint of a harquebus and used to set fire to a nearby field of straw.
After it quickly burned, the captain moved into the clearing with his men and
horses. Thus, when the fire started by the enemy reached the Spaniards there
was no longer any field to burn and the opponents' scheme was ruined. . . .

By this time — now it was later in the day — the sun was extremely hot and
the Spaniards . . . were afflicted by the heat and by their chain mail armor,

.ch becomes very hot under the strength of the sun. They were also notably .red from thirst, for the river was half a league away. Their only relief was to carry the lead shot in their mouths, a practice Spaniards rely on in these lands. Although the enemy had their refuge in the shade of the trees, they were nevertheless so fatigued that they ordered their women to bring them jugs of water. . . .

Then the enemy began to withdraw, for they were being lured away by their desire to enjoy a part of the spoils. . . . They tore everything to pieces and killed many of the horses and mules. Night finally began to fall. . . . [The captain] and his soldiers decided that once it was dark they would release some of the wounded horses. Once the horses were free they would run to the river. . . . The captain was certain that when the enemy heard the pounding of the horses' hooves they would think that the Spaniards were headed for the river, tired from thirst, whereupon the troop of Indians would fire on them. Thus, the Spaniards would have a good opportunity to take off.

This plan worked, and the captain and his small band of soldiers escaped. Meanwhile, the other Spanish soldiers had returned to the villa of Sinaloa with most of the Indian allies. They thought that Captain Hurdaide was dead, overwhelmed by the Yaquis.

Father Pérez de Ribas was at Mochicahui, the main pueblo of the Zuaques, when he received a messenger who advised that all the area priests meet in Sinaloa. They were in grave danger. Father Pérez de Ribas met with eight other priests, including Father Martín Pérez.

When a soldier, dusty and bloody, rode into the villa's plaza, he handed Father Pérez a piece of paper that had been "used as wadding in a harquebus." It said, "God forgive those men who abandoned me and thus placed the whole province in danger. Although wounded, I and the other soldiers who stayed with me are alive. We continue traveling slowly due to the fatigue of the horses and the wounded. In order to avoid an uprising in the province as a result of the news that those other soldiers might have brought, I am sending posthaste this soldier, who has been very loyal to me."

The captain had requested pardon from the church for his deserting soldiers, and Pérez de Ribas agreed. The governor of Vizcaya, however, was not so easily appeased. He ordered an investigation of the soldiers' conduct. Captain Hurdaide suggested that the matter be overlooked. His reasoning was that the Indian allies had also deserted, and if the governor punished the Spanish soldiers, the army might lose its Indian allies when it needed all the help it could get in the perilous future. The captain knew he would have to return to make some kind of peace with the Yaqui nation. The governor considered the arguments and agreed to drop the investigation.

An uneasy year followed. The Spaniards were reluctant to face the battlefield again.

Then something surprising happened. The Yaquis asked for peace.

Such a thing was unheard of, but the Spaniards spent little time in speculation. Perhaps the Yaquis were amazed at the Spaniards' fighting ability. Perhaps they had heard rumors circulated by Hurdaide that he was amassing reinforcements by sea. Or maybe they thought Hurdaide's escape from capture was so miraculous that there must have been special magic in it.

Yet while many Yaquis wanted peace, some hoped for more war. They had a new idea: they would take the Spaniards' own machetes and then the bravest Yaquis would throw themselves under the horses' legs and cut their hamstrings. When the Spanish rider fell to the ground, he would be helpless because of the weight of his armor. Indian allies carried news of this tactic to the captain.

Captain Hurdaide was a tough man. He was a fighter, but also a thinker, a strategist. He used whatever means he could to intimidate Indians. In 1615 he met with the leaders of the various tribes surrounding Yaqui territory. He explained how he would destroy the Yaquis, killing the men and enslaving the women and children. He would annihilate them all. He would lead three contingents of Indian allies; they would spread across the land, trampling the crops and burning the homes. Spanish ships would attack the lower pueblos near the sea. Soldiers and their armored horses would flood from the ships in great waves of metal, gunpowder, smoke, and sabers. When the battle was over, he promised the allied Indian leaders, they could have their pick of slaves and whatever vengeance they wanted on the Yaquis—a final payback for all the years the Yaquis had raided other tribes.

It's not surprising that the Yaquis heard about this. It's exactly what Captain Hurdaide wanted. The Yaquis counciled among themselves, debating, considering, wondering. There were many, of course, who laughed at the threat. They wanted action.

But the Yaquis had changed leadership and were now governed by a man who wanted peace with the Jesuit missionaries. The Mayo Indians reported quite favorably on conditions they found in other missions.

But the Yaquis needed to see these conditions firsthand. One of the problems was that in order for a messenger to travel between Yaqui country and the missions, he had to pass through the land of the Teguecos, who hated the Yaquis. The Teguecos had previously sent envoys to the Yaquis only to have their representatives murdered.

A man named Conibomeai, a Yaqui leader, suggested that a woman travel as an envoy to the Mayos. She herself was a leader. Her name is unknown. She was to ascertain the real fate of the Yaquis if they surrendered. Would they be killed anyway?

As she crossed the Río Yaqui, she told the other leaders that if she hadn't returned in four days, they should consider her dead.

"God inspired this woman to walk eleven leagues," recorded Pérez de Ribas, "and to enter the midst of her enemies. She reached the Mayo and met with the two caciques, to whom she gave the message. . . . They heard the message of peace with pleasure. They told the woman to tell the Yaqui that they would help, provided the Yaqui really and truly were pursuing peace and friendship. . . . Because these peoples were constantly at war, they trusted each other very little. Then the two Mayo caciques sent the Yaqui woman back. For her greater safety they and some of their people accompanied her so that others would not kill her before she reached safety."

When she returned, the Yaqui leaders gathered in conference. The first test had been passed. She was not dead. The Mayos seemed to be speaking the truth. So they decided to send her back, along with two other women who had been born Mayo but had married a Yaqui man named Otatavo. They were to request, again, that a message of peace be forwarded to Hurdaide.

The Spanish captain was pleased to hear this, of course, and requested a meeting with the Yaqui leaders. The Yaqui women stayed at a villa in Sinaloa for several days and received gifts of horses, blankets, and clothing.

The women traveled safely back to Yaqui country, carrying additional presents for the leaders: blankets, small items, and more horses. The Spaniards and the Yaqui leaders met at the borders of Mayo and Yaqui country, facing each other uneasily. The terms of the treaty began to be hammered out.

The peace treaty required that the Yaquis give up all horses and weapons captured during the last battle. The Yaquis were also to keep peace with other tribes, such as the Mayos. And they had to hand over the two Ocoroni fugitives, who had, in some ways, started all the fighting.

Father Pérez de Ribas reported that the captain treated the women messengers to gifts—they were dressed "like the women of [central] Mexico, with *huipiles* [tunics] or blouses and shifts of bright colors and feathers, a novelty that they had never seen before."

The Yaquis requested that missionaries be sent to Yaqui country, without a military escort. Captain Hurdaide promised that no Spanish army would dominate Yaqui lands and that if another tribe made war against the Yaquis, the Spaniards would fight for the Yaquis. He gave each Yaqui leader a number of fine horses, clothing, and food for their return journey.

The two Ocoronis, Lautaro and Babilomo, were caught and bound and sent to the Spanish authorities, who judged them guilty of rebellion and sentenced them to hang.

Father Pérez de Ribas wrote, "God Our Lord willed to show them the light to recognize their crimes and to ask for pardon and Holy Baptism at the hour of their deaths. . . . This time the devil came out quite badly, and the commotion and storm with which he had attempted to destroy Christianity in Sinaloa was dispelled."

Oh, My Grandfather

From the journal of Father Pérez de Ribas:

No one can deny that atheists are the most hopeless and lost people in the world, and also the most distant from divine light, for they close their minds and ears to the principal truth of all divine doctrine, the basis of eternal salvation. . . .

Let us turn now to the barbarous peoples who are the subject of this history. I paid close attention to the matter of idolatry . . . and it is accurate to state that whereas traces of formal idolatry existed among some of these peoples, others did not have any knowledge of God, nor of any deity, not even a false one; nor was there explicit worship of a Lord who held dominion over the world. . . .

The devil frequently spoke to the Indians when they were gentiles, appearing to them in the form of animals, fish, or serpents; he has not forgotten how successful he was in assuming this same shape to cause the downfall of our first mother. The Indians greatly respected and feared him whenever he appeared, and as a title of respect they called him "Grandfather." They did so without distinguishing whether he was creature or creator. Even though they recognized the shape of the animal or serpent in which the devil appeared to them, painting it in their own fashion or sometimes erecting a stone or pole as an idol, they clearly did not seem to recognize a deity or supreme power of the universe.

I will write here about the sorcerers and their role and customs. It was very common practice among all these nations to have such preachers. . . . [They preached sermons] at the outset of a war, during peace talks with another nation or with the Spaniards, or when they celebrated a victory or the taking of enemy heads. On these occasions the old principales and the sorcerers would meet at the house or ramada of the cacique. They would be seated around a torch, where they would proceed to light some of their tobacco-filled reeds, which they would then pass around to smoke. Then the Indian who held the greatest authority would stand up, and from his standing position he would chant the beginning of his sermon. He would start by walking very slowly around the plaza of the pueblo, continuing his sermon and raising the tone of his voice, shouting so that the entire pueblo could hear him from their bonfires and houses. This circling of the plaza and sermon would take more or less half an hour, depending on the preacher. When this was done he would return to his seat, where his companions would welcome him with great acclaim. Each one would express this individually, and if the preacher was an old man, which they usually are, the response went like this: "You have spoken and advised us well, my grandfather. My heart is one with yours." If the person congratulating him were an old man, he would say, "My older or younger brother, my heart feels and speaks what you have said." Then they would honor him with another toast and round of tobacco. Next, another orator would get up and give his sermon in the same manner, spending another half an hour circling the plaza.

The usual epilogue of these sermons exhorted all members of the pueblo, young and old alike, invoking them in terms of kinship, saying, "my grandfathers, my fathers, my older and younger brothers, sons and daughters of my brothers, let us be of one heart and mind." This is how they concluded their sermons. They truly had a great capacity to move people to do whatever they wished, be it good or evil. For this reason, so that they might promote the divine word and Christian customs, they are still permitted to deliver sermons even after they are baptized and converted. To accomplish this they repeat many times, "The word of God has reached our lands; we are no longer who we were before."

Note: Pérez de Ribas also commented that the sorcerers wore pouches of animal fur in which they kept colored pebbles and other items. Upon baptism they were required to hand over these sacred medicine bags.

We Came This Way

Much has been studied and written concerning how these peoples
reached the New World, separated as it is from the Old by such
immense seas. . . . [The most likely idea is that] these people arrived
from Asia overland to the north or crossed some narrow stretch of
sea that was easy to cross and remains as yet undiscovered. . . .

More than a few times I very carefully questioned the eldest
and most intelligent of these Indians, asking whence they had
come and when they or their ancestors had settled the places that
they presently occupy. Every one of them consistently responded
that they had come from the north, abandoning places that
they had held and settled. These had been taken from
them in warfare and subsequently occupied by those
other nations that had overcome them. . . .

These people say that the Spaniards are the only ones
who came from the east.
—*Father Andrés Pérez de Ribas*, History of the Triumphs of
Our Holy Faith amongst the Most Barbarous and
Fierce Peoples of the New World.

We came this way
we came this way
which has not yet been discovered   this way
by a Dane across a narrow arm of mast or sea

this way we came

our skin is red-orange from the sun & wild mulberry juice   our skin
is mysterious, scattered with ice-colored clouds of cottonwood seeds
this way our skin is a continent
journeying over mapless water

this way

we are beautiful   in our ears, long indigo blue loops of cotton
& white pearls, aqua-pink shells   this way
we always hear the sea   & in our noses like green crescent moons:
bright stones   our hair loose & straight as rain

we came

skirted in woven willow, or fibers of maguey, fine cotton   this way
we came naked
or in blue capes, skins of night jaguars & green-eyed stars
this way

we became

animals in the spiral breaths of mountain roars,
this way into the rivers' dark-mouthed centers   we came
discovered, discovering thick forests of ebony, brazil
& rosewood where birds cannot fly

this way

we heard the alligators dreaming of carving
sky into flesh shapes so we came to ford rivers
with loud talking   this way we are called   People Who Shout
Across the River   it is our way

we came

to our enemies & killed them   this way: with flint knives & spikes
        embedded
in the ground   with poisoned arrows with blood-splattered war clubs,
        spears
with men drinking the juice of the mescal plant & dancing
this way we impale our enemies' heads on poles   we insult them

this way

everyone fears us so we are safe
this way we live when it floods: we build houses in the trees
dreaming of red stars falling into our hands
this way we enter the water of our souls

we came

to the ocean to harvest sea kelp, pearls   with nets of sisal fiber
we fish this way   there are deer, wild pig, rabbits, iguanas which we
        hunt

this way: where there is water in the hollow of trees we find them
& break their jaws, stringing them together

this way

we can hunt many hours with fresh meat & later, with our fingers
we probe for small stones in the iguana's stomach
these are good medicine
the *hechiceros* suck out thorns, sticks, or pebbles   it goes this way out

we came

to corn, beans, squash   from the north we came, carrying tobacco
& pieces of coral, silver in medicine bags, small knots of scalps,
animal or human   we passed this way with our youngest & oldest
from far north   only the Spaniards came from the southeast

they came

with gifts of smallpox & slavery   this way they came
with spotted horses & striped blankets which we wore this way
over the arm which pointed north
when they asked where there were riches of gold or silver   away

that way

we said, go north   there you will find what you seek   far north
across the narrow sea   follow the Red Road into Asia,   go back
far until you come to Spain   go home   *that* way   go *that*
          way
& leave us for we have come this way   this way

we came.

Note: From 1733 to 1741, Vitus Bering explored the Arctic and rediscovered the strait of water later named after him. Earlier, in 1648, Semyon Dezhnev recorded his discovery of the same body of water, but the materials were lost in the archives. In one book I read that Chinese junks were seen in the Gulf of California by Spanish explorers, who also reported that there had been centuries of trading between the two cultures. I have been unable to substantiate that claim in my research.

In the Land of the Restless Yaquis

"At this point in the conversion of this nation [1619] the number of
baptized children reached forty-nine hundred, with
three thousand baptized adults."
—*Father Pérez de Ribas*

Padre Tomás Basilio served for more than thirty years as a priest in Yaqui territory. One day, at twilight, he rested outside his house. An arrow shot out of the gathering darkness and struck him in the chest. The arrow, which was poisoned in the old-fashioned way of the Yaquis, bounced off his skin, leaving him with only a small wound. If the arrow had been freshly poisoned, he would have died. Instead, the greatest worry was infection. Immediately, the Yaqui leader don Ignacio knelt by the padre's side and sucked out whatever poison remained. Don Ignacio spat out the blood and grit, then rinsed out his mouth with fresh water.

When the padre was resting comfortably, don Ignacio found the arrow and then decided to find its owner. The crowd that had gathered outside the padre's house was very helpful, pointing out the arrow's many owners—all who had won it and lost it during games of *patoli* and *canuelas*. Although the padre couldn't tell one arrow from another, the Yaquis could identify the marks and colorings as belonging to one person. Eventually, they found the maker, then traced the ownership until they knew who had shot the arrow.

The man had already escaped into the woods, but don Ignacio and his men followed the faint tracks and broken twigs until they found him. He was sent to Captain Hurdaide. When questioned, he admitted the attempt on the padre's life. His reason? The padre wouldn't let him keep a woman he wanted. He had hoped to kill the padre and incite an uprising against the Spaniards. His uncle had urged him to take the first step toward rebellion by killing Padre Basilio.

This uncle had fled to the Nebome nation, two hundred miles away, and was returned by a guard of Nebomes. On the way back to the captain, the uncle managed to grab a poisoned arrow from his guards and inflict a wound on himself. A priest from the Mayos was brought to the dying man in case he wanted to repent before his death, but he refused. He died within twenty-four hours without saying a word.

His nephew, the one who had shot the arrow at the padre, was sentenced to be hung and died after confessing to the priest, who felt that this awarded the hanged man a better death.

From 1621 to 1623, more than thirty thousand Yaquis were baptized. Still, the priests were bothered by the people's continuing belief in the old ways.

A Yaqui woman who had been baptized pointed to the mountains. "There, Padre, are our mountains, which we know and hold in reverence. Every tree and rock is held sacred by us."

Father Pérez de Ribas wrote in his book, "The old women certified that the devil appeared to them in the form of dogs, toads, coyotes, and snakes—forms that correspond to what he is."

At night, the medicine men, *hechiceros* (or sorcerers, as Pérez de Ribas called them), flew through the air after their dances with demons in the high mountain wilderness. A padre visited one pueblo and sternly scolded the people for believing in this.

An hechicero came forward, arms crossed over his chest. "Father, don't bother to assemble us [for a sermon], because more or less half of the people in the pueblo [which was very large] are just like us."

A woman hechicero nodded. "You have not been killed, Padre, because you have brought *some* good to the pueblos." The others behind her whispered. She added, "And your prayers, which you say at mass, have kept you safe."

So in spite of the padres' continuing efforts and their tallying the numbers of baptized Indians, not all was well.

The priests thought that the sorcerers were manipulating the people. For example, when one pueblo was stricken with smallpox, an Indian man "boasted that he had brought on this illness" and demanded gifts before he would stop the plague. The priests confronted the man and asked him why he couldn't kill them if he was so powerful. The answer was that because the priests say mass, they are powerful. The priests continually preached against the hechiceros, thereby undermining the status of the medicine men and women and also destroying the ancient fabric of Yaqui society.

One hechicero began to talk against Christianity and those already baptized. In secret meetings, where tobacco was ceremonially smoked, he urged people not to be so gullible, not to believe what the priests said.

He asserted that Christianity was pure myth—that there were not in heaven the privileges of which the Indians were told by the padres.

Under the shade of the river willows, he jabbed the air with long fingers. "Your soul does not go to heaven. Your soul is buried in your body when you die. There is nothing more than this life. So why be so pious? Why just one wife when you love many? Why have you thrown away the *ollas* of liquor and stopped dancing around the fires? Why have you let our enemies encroach on our lands? Why? Why?

"I'll tell you why! Because you have listened to those liars, the padres, who are not men enough to love a woman or drink strong like a Yaqui! Have they ever fought in war, stabbing an enemy between the ribs? Have they ever hunted a deer? No! They say: *Don't do this, don't do that!* for all the gay things in life. And all the work, oh, they make you do it for them! It's true that you are stupid Yaquis, those of you who let them tell you how to live like white men!"

Then he pointed to the riverbank. The crowd turned to look. An old man stood there, his face heavily lined, his hair white and long. He spoke to the people.

"Take a good look at me, I am an old man. Tomorrow after I bathe in the river you will see that I am young. The same thing can happen to all of you."

The next day, the people lined the river waiting for the old man to appear again. The crowd was thicker than the day before because the news had traveled throughout the pueblos. Everyone wanted to see, and believe, the old magic.

"Look!"

"There he is!"

People stood on their toes, straining to see.

A young man stood on the riverbank where the old one had been. He wore a long black cloak and carried a shield.

"Oh! He's so handsome!"

"He is young!"

"If I could be so young again . . ."

The hechicero signaled to a group of drummers. He urged the people to dance in the old ways. Their eyes sparkling, the men and women turned toward the hechicero. When they glanced back for another view of the young man, he was gone. The men danced, throwing up dust with their pounding heels. That night, the old songs were sung and the men raised their arms, shaking their fists at the night.

In the priest's house, he shoved a chair against the door and, fingering his cross, began to pray.

Captain Hurdaide was notified of the incident and rode with his soldiers to the pueblo.

He ordered that the hechicero be brought to him for questioning.

"This was no trick," argued the *hechicero*, "it was true. An old crow told me what to do and say. I saw him in the branches of a cottonwood tree. He wore a black robe."

"It was the devil!" The padre crossed himself.

The hechicero shrugged.

Captain Hurdaide spoke. "As we rode into the pueblo, someone shot two arrows at us. What do you know about this?"

The hechicero's eyes widened. This was a different matter. "¡N-nada!"

"Are you certain?"

The hechicero assessed the situation. "It must be the work of the devil. You're right, Padre. I was tricked! That old crow told me to kill the padres, burn the churches, and throw the church bells into the river. Also, I was supposed to kill you, Captain, and all the white men. But as you see, I did none of this. I am innocent!"

The Captain had other ideas, however, and sentenced the man to death by hanging, along with several other men.

Divine mercy disabused and prepared them well for death, for they acknowledged their guilt and confessed their sins with great remorse, particularly the delinquent principal cacique. His hope was to see his son in heaven, because he had died with Holy Baptism.

After the punishment had been carried out and the scandal removed, the Yaqui along the entire river were quieted.

Vildósola's Decrees

1740

In *Cycles of Conquest*, Edward Spicer wrote that the Spanish soldier Vildósola, having defeated the whole Yaqui army at Otamcahui, the Hill of the Bones, instituted several new decrees:

1. No Indian is allowed to leave the pueblo without permission from the missionaries.
2. Indians shall be impressed for forced labor on the haciendas and in the mines.
3. Indians must pray every day in all the mission pueblos.

Once again, the missions, haciendas, and mines were in control of the Indians' lives. The only things that had changed were that soldiers now occupied the territory and that Vildósola was in charge, enjoying great power among the mine owners, the hacienda gentlemen, and the priests, who attempted to recover the prosperity of the old days. Only twenty-three thousand Yaquis remained in their ancestral lands. Many had died, and some, who were experienced as miners, worked in the mines in Durango, Chihuahua, Sonora, and Sinaloa. Other Yaquis had left to work the fields in surrounding towns and haciendas.

In 1746, Vildósola was accused of mishandling government funds and forced to leave his office.

Rabbit and Coyote

One day Coyote was walking along, sniffing for beetles. He was so thin his ribs sang in the wind.

Then he saw Rabbit.

"I'm going to eat you!" shouted Coyote.

Rabbit twitched his ears. "I've got a better idea. My friends are cooking a lot of food. Wait here and I'll get some for you."

Rabbit hopped away.

Coyote waited, singing little songs to himself. He was daydreaming about all the food he'd soon be eating. His stomach growled. Maybe some nice boiled corn. Tortillas wrapped around bits of juicy chicken. And a furry rabbit for desert.

After a while, though, he wondered what had become of Rabbit, so he followed his trail.

He found Rabbit leaning against a cliff. Small rocks rolled down, clinking against other fallen stones.

"Why are you standing there like that?" asked Coyote.

"The cliff is about to fall down. I'm holding it up. I'm so glad to see you, primo. If you'll take my place here—yes, like that, just push your paws up against the cliff—I'll go get our food and some more help from mi familia."

Coyote grunted, pushing against the cliff. It was hot, and sweat rolled down from between his ears, dripping off the tip of his nose. He was feeling weaker. His front legs were shaking from the strain. With each breath, he felt his stomach rattling around inside like a dried pinto bean.

All around him, the desert was quiet except for the buzzing of flies. The minutes stretched into an hour. Coyote was trembling.

Finally he didn't care anymore. Let the cliff fall down on him. Let this hard life end.

He jumped away, waiting for the rock to tumble down, crushing him. But nothing happened!

Rabbit had tricked Coyote again.

•

Note: This is an old Yaqui story that has traveled all over the continent. The same story can be found as far north as central Washington State.

Indian Vices

(IN THE PERSONA OF FATHER OCH)

By nature Indians are very lazy and sworn enemies of work.
They prefer to suffer hunger than to fatigue themselves
with agriculture. Therefore, they must be forced to do this by their
superiors. With six industrious Europeans one can do more
in one day than fifty Indians.
—*Joseph Och*, Missionary in Sonora: Travel Reports
of Joseph Och, S.J., 1755–1767

Mining: The Indian is naked, swinging
quarter to half hundredweight steel-edged crowbars.
He climbs beams with notches set step by step,
carrying ore in plaited baskets
on his shoulders.
They are given one half-bushel of maize per week.
This is their payment unless they have a family—
then they are given two half-bushels.

*Two men using wheelbarrows could haul out
more than can thirty lazy Indians
working an entire day.*

Natural resources: They are naked, with only a loincloth.
Otherwise they would steal valuable ore.
Instead they laugh
when their hair is thick with dusted gold
so that they look like ugly yellow-haired creatures.
Their hair is long and they secrete fragments
of ore there, wrapping their hair up
like a turban. You can no more trust them
than you would a Turk.

*Gold and silver ore varies.
Some is very heavy, pure
silver spiked, as it were,*

with silver nails.
The completely black
very heavy ores
are considered the richest.

Processing: The Indian washes his hair
several times a day, sluicing water
over his long hair, letting the silver fall
into a bowl which he then strains,
keeping more silver.
Then again, the Indian must relieve himself
and he hides behind a bush,
thereby stealing more ore
in a most despicable way.

Some can be reduced by fire . . .
or be broken up
and placed into a clay oven
. . . with molten lead,
until . . . the lead has amalgamated
with the silver.
Pebbles and slag float on top
and are skinned off
with hoes and the lead heated
with a double fire
until it becomes light and frothy
like glass.
This froth is removed in heaps;
what remains is pure silver.

The waste product: When the Indian dies,
perhaps careless at work, he is wrapped in a horse blanket.
Thread from deer or plant fiber
is used to sew him up.
It is heathen, this practice
of putting bows and arrows,
small bowls, and other things
in the grave. Instead, I pull the bell rope

and they are pleased at the songs
and lighted tapers
on the altar of the whitewashed church.
They die when they want to,
saying they are only journeying
to the next village.

They have many vices
which I have discovered
and abolished, including the throwing
of patterned sticks,
which is like gambling.
They would rather lie on blankets
in the bushes, throwing these sticks
against the rough wool to muffle the sound,
than work in the fields
or in the mines which are very near,
nor do they think of tomorrow
and the profit that must be made,
whether it is gold, silver, maize,
or their heathenish souls.

Red at Bacum

MEXICO, 1868

One of García Morales' colonels at Cocorit accepted the plea
for peace of a group of six hundred [Yaqui] men, women, and
children. He asked them to turn over their arms and when a few
were given up, he let 150 of the prisoners go and imprisoned the
remaining 450 in the church at Bacum. He held ten leaders as
hostages, saying that if there were any attempts at escape he
would shoot all ten. During the night he trained his artillery on
the door of the church. There was a disturbance during the
night. The colonel ordered the ten leaders shot and, as a fire
broke out within the church, the artillery shelled the doorway.
The result was that some 120 Indians [Yaquis] were massacred.
—*Edward Spicer*, Cycles of Conquest

1

there are red clouds
of smoke
and splinters of bone

there are green palm
fronds smoldering above
the shattered altar

there are nails exploding
out the end of cooked fingers
there are 120

ways they died, alone, together
in front of the cross   praying
or spitting at it   skin sizzling

red mouths blood gun fire
red wine sacramental robes
red falling   red shredded

2

the next day hummingbirds
took the hair from human skulls
to weave nests

for tiny shells, heartbeats
they like anything red
fire

embroidery thread on white cotton
a small gold cross still glowing hot
among Bacum ashes

Gifted with a Spirited Imagination

In 1821, the Plan of Iguala stated that "all inhabitants of New Spain, without distinction between Europeans, Africans, or Indians," were to be declared citizens of the monarchy. After Mexico won its War of Independence from Spain later that year, it continued with the plan, setting up provincial governments in each newly formed state to ensure compliance with one of the most important aspects of statehood: taxation of citizens.

The Yaquis became taxable, along with their rich riverbottom lands. In 1825, when the Yaquis refused to pay taxes, saying that they had never had to before, soldiers were sent to enforce payment. Small groups of Yaquis fought, encouraged by Father Pedro Leyva, who lived at the mission in Cocorit. As the Mexican soldiers and Yaquis clashed, more Indians joined in the fight. Two thousand men, armed with bows and arrows, stood ready for battle under the command of Juan Banderas, himself a Yaqui.

He wanted an independent Indian state in northern Mexico. He sought reinforcements from the Mayos, Pimas, and Opatas. He was successful in organizing a large army of Indians from diverse tribes and condemned the two hundred Yaquis who joined the Mexican army as traitors.

Banderas's battle symbol was the Virgin of Guadalupe, the Indian Virgin who had appeared to a peasant, Juan Diego, in 1531. She wore a beautiful sky-blue robe and let her long black hair fall loosely to the ground. Around her, the smell of roses perfumed the air.

It was said that in Mexico, God was a woman, an Indian woman, and she became the cry of those who wanted an Indian land. Banderas carried her banner to war, where the air stank of sweat, blood, and cordite.

Once again the Spaniards—now Mexicans—were forced out of the area. The government sought peace, and Banderas agreed to the power of the state, hoping that his authority would be autonomous. The Mexican government pardoned him for his part in the revolution and appointed him captain general. Ironically, his post was supported with tax funds.

Then, in a series of reforms, the government abolished his position, although it allowed him and others to receive a life stipend. The pueblos were ordered to maintain their own system of government by electing officials. School became compulsory. Land had to be platted and surveyed, with title given to owners, and the land had to be distributed fairly. The Yaquis had resisted all previous efforts to individualize their land.

Banderas again organized resistance. In 1832 he joined forces with the Opatas and seized control of Yaqui pueblos.

In his *Cycles of Conquest*, Edward Spicer notes that Ignacio Zúñiga, commandant of the Mexican soldiers in Pitic, described Banderas as follows:

> The chief of these last two [uprisings] has been the Indian Banderas, General of the nation, a man of genius for directing and enthusing his followers, gifted with a spirited imagination, with eloquence and with a rare talent, with which he could have accomplished many more evils if his plans had been favored. . . . He conceived the plan of crowning himself king and of bringing about a general reconciliation among all the tribes for establishing his monarchy and sustaining the cause of the Indians against the whites. To this end he sent envoys to the other tribes, charging them with artful and flattering messages to invite them to join cause with him. He reminded all of them of that which should move them most, that is to say, the question of the lands: he painted our race as ambitious and dominating, and made use of the [existing] hatreds, grudges, and [desire for] vengeance, passions common to all the Indians, to excite them to agree to the consolidation of his military movements. . . . This caudillo [chieftain], courageous and ambitious, was shot at Arispe, leaving a memory among his people which perhaps will contribute strongly to the development of his doctrines, which can one day be regrettable. They have been planted; if they are left to germinate, propagate, and grow, will they not produce their fruit? . . . [T]he doctrines of this bandit, and the great riches of all kinds which he distributed to the Indians will be for a long time the food of frequent rebellions and raids; since he succeeded in convincing them that they are the legitimate proprietors of whatever there is; and he taught them to live by robbing, something they will not forget easily, if punishment be not exemplary and prompt, following immediately the crime.

Banderas was executed in 1833.

Legal Persecution

In Spicer's *Cycles of Conquest*, he quotes from the Constitution of the state of Sonora, September 1873:

> Article IV. To deprive the Yaqui and Mayo tribes of the rights of citizenship while they maintain the anomalous organization that they have in their towns and rancherías, but allowing the enjoyment [of those rights] to individuals of the same tribes who reside in the organized pueblos of the state.

In other words, only those Yaquis who lived in government-organized towns would be allowed citizenship in a land they had called their own for thousands of years.

From the state legislature's report, 1880, as quoted by Spicer:

> Thus, little by little, and with the passage of time, the dominions of such tribes [Opatas, Seris, Papagos] as populate Sonora have been narrowed, to give place to civilization and to form a people which if it is not the most learned in the Republic, is at least not the last.
>
> Only the Yaquis and Mayos have been able to remain obstinate in their savage life, occupying a great extent of land on both the best rivers which the state possesses, masters of the most fertile lands, without any organization, without obedience to either authority or laws, completely removed from obedience to all government, and what is more, constantly making collection of war materials, as though preparing for an armed struggle, and committing continuous robberies and assassinations against the interests and persons of those who get within their reach. . . .
>
> Is it perhaps that the Mexican government is so weak that it cannot reduce these savages to order, requiring them to live like the other inhabitants, and making them begin the life of civilization?

Mexican Gifts

The Yaquis, after several battles, suffered defeat by General Carbo in 1886. Two hundred Yaquis died, and two thousand became prisoners of war. Many were women and children.

Reprisals included deportation, enslavement, rape, murder, and starvation.

Those who managed to escape into the Bacatete Mountains suffered from lack of food. Eventually, some families straggled into the eight Yaqui towns and gave themselves up. Out of a population of fourteen thousand Yaquis farming on the rivers, four thousand surrendered to the authorities of the Mexican administration. They were given ten centavos per person per day and seeds for planting.

A Mexican reporter (quoted by Spicer in *Cycles of Conquest*) commented that "now this was the beginning of the great and humanitarian work: the civilizing and incorporating [of the Yaquis] into the common mass of citizens of the Republic."

Letters: Word Bullets

In *Cycles of Conquest*, Spicer tells about the verbal confrontations between the Yaquis and the Mexican government. President Díaz wrote to General Torres, around 1897, that

> we should not be tranquil until we see each Indian with his plow in his hand, behind a team of oxen, cultivating the fields.

A Mexican writer penned this comment:

> In short, whatever resource it was humanly possible to use to move and convince the Indians, such was exerted to the utmost to domesticate the wild beast.

General Torres to the Yaquis:

> Don't believe that the parcels of land which now have been delivered to you are all that the Supreme Government will give you. Should one of you come and say to me: "Sir, I have sons. We lack land to cultivate."—you shall have what you need; but now, seeing that scarcely a tenth part of that which you possess is cultivated, you must agree that you have more than enough to cover your necessities.

Reported Colonel Manuel Gil:

> A curious phenomenon: of the Indians who returned to occupy the river, ninety per cent had spent years practicing the civilized life in the towns of the state. Arriving in the Yaqui, they replaced, with pleasure, their delicious coffee with pinole; their shoes with sandals; and the women, keeping in the bottoms of their trunks, silks, laces, and stockings, returned joyously to bare feet and primitive clothes. The clothing of the children was reduced to its simplest expression.

The old Yaqui men told Father Beltrán that in the old days there had been no Mexicans in Yaqui country. They wondered when the Mexicans would leave. And, incidentally, they said, there's no need for priests, either.

From the village of Cocorit, part of a letter sent to General Torres in 1899, signed by "the eight Yaqui towns":

> What we want is that all whites and troops get out. If they go for good, then there will be peace; if not we declare war. Because the peace which we signed in Ortiz was on the condition that troops and whites would leave and this they have still not done; on the contrary, in place of complying they have taken away [our] arms. Certainly now you are behind all the business, and we have no blame for all the misfortunes that there are.

Replied General Torres:

> You are not the eight towns of the Yaqui, but can be considered only as a gang of evil-doers, which, not desiring peace or honorable work and not recognizing the benefits you have received from the Government, have got together to commit robberies and assassinations.

The Mexican military historian Troncoso reported in 1905 that the

> Yaquis were inherently warlike and that the women particularly could not be changed and that they instilled hostility into their children. . . . The solution was the separation of mothers and children.

In 1900 a Colonel Penna wrote:

> Convinced that it should not concern itself with the question of justice in giving pieces of land to the Indians, that matter having been well debated and perfectly demonstrated that that is not what the Indians wanted, since they have abandoned their lands to follow rebellion and their titles have served as wadding for their guns, it is clear to be seen that their sole desire is but to drive out the Mexicans; the land in the form in which they have received it does not interest them. Their reasoning in this particular is the following: "God gave the river to all the Yaquis, not one piece to each."

In 1900 there were 7,606 Yaquis and 3,639 colonists in northern Mexico.

Another Trail of Tears

THE MASSACRE OF MAZOCOBA

In 1900, General Torres battled the rebel Yaquis in the Bacatete Mountains and killed four hundred men. Many Yaquis committed suicide. Over a thousand women and children were forced to march down the trail; most died on the way. This is called the Massacre of Mazocoba.

Only eighteen Mexican soldiers were killed and sixty-two wounded. Thirty-five guns were taken from the Yaquis after their surrender.

The Yaqui survivors were deported to haciendas throughout Sonora, where they worked as slaves.

General Torres issued a series of regulations:

1. Yaquis must settle only in certain, specified areas.
2. Yaquis must associate only with other Yaquis on the haciendas.
3. Once a month, every Yaqui must check in with authorities.
4. Yaquis must carry registration papers at all times or face jail.
5. Yaquis will be observed in every settlement by the authorities.

The general received large amounts of Yaqui land, which he incorporated into his own hacienda. A friend of his, Rafael Izabal, suggested routine raids and removal of Yaquis in 1903. Yaquis were deported north and south. By 1907, Yaquis were a cash commodity, selling for sixty pesos a head to the owners of henequen plantations in Yucatán and sugar fields in Oaxaca. Five thousand Yaquis were shoved into boats, sailed down the west coast, and then marched to the east coast, where they were once again put on boats to the Yucatán Peninsula.

Note: It was about this time that my grandparents left Mexico.

PART TWO

Cuentos de Mi Familia /
Stories of My Family

The following section contains stories of my
immediate family and my mythical ancient family.
In most cases, the two sets of families converge in
the spirit of storytelling, in the powerful beating of
the female heart. Threads from the rebozos, or
shawls, of La Morena, Tonantzin, Tequatlasupe,
and La Llorona intertwine among the flashy
dresses and ordinary blue jeans that the women in
these stories wear. Some of the stories are written
as poems. Some are told in paintings. And some,
such as the story of the fictional Esperanza sisters,
create the kin I could have had if all the Yaqui
women had been able to tell their own stories.

Coyote Woman

Once there was a man named Manuel the Weak, or, in Yaqui, Mangwe Wakira. He had large, dusty feet which he shuffled in the dirt of his fields as he hoed and watered, his back bent like a turtle's. The cuffs of his white cotton pants were dark with earth and bright with the seedlings of squash and tomatoes that sprouted there. His shoulders were thin, too sharp for birds to perch on with their curious eyes, and they flew over him, wondering if he was plant or animal.

Every day he lived alone, at the edge of his fields, and at night the stars glowed on the sea, and the seedlings in his cuffs stretched their roots, tearing the cloth. Every day he lived alone and every night.

Nearby lived a Yaqui woman who was also a witch. All Yaqui women are beautiful, but she was beautiful even in the dark. Maybe all women are beautiful in the dark, but the darkness was in her beauty. She was a witch.

At night she went into the desert and removed her clothes. Her shoulders were straight and her feet were small. Her hair was like black water; her eyes darted quickly, seeking the broken bits of moon, small tufts of mouse hair, the shattered bones of birds. She sat on the earth and glared at the man's hut made of sticks, and the single-man smell of him disturbed her. There were no edges of woman around him, no smells of good cooking or clothes pounded clean in the river. There was no wildness, either, that might have pleased or aroused her. There was just the neglectfulness of a male when he has only himself to think about. The dirt under his toenails made her eyes narrow, and his thin neck made her long for an ax and a chopping block.

She watched his dark hut as the moon rose and fell, and her arms shook from the weight of the night. She watched him when he crawled out of his house and stood up, stretching and grunting, sunrise causing the seedlings in his cuffs to twist their leaves toward the light. He shuffled toward the river and knelt down, throwing handfuls of cold water on his face, snuffling and slurping, then wiping his face on his forearm. He turned, stood by a willow, and urinated, the stream of water running down between his toes.

He ate something gray and greasy. He lifted his heavy head and peered at the sun, and she saw his brown eyes, soft with resignation, the eyes of a burro. And then he worked, shuffling his big, dusty feet through the earth, as if he were sinking into another layer of himself.

At last she would get up, brush off the soil from her nakedness, and go home to a fine meal of chilies and maize and fresh tortillas with beans simmered in pork. Witches are good cooks. They know about appetites of all kinds and are careful with ingredients.

At night, the man would go into his hut again, a hut not much bigger than himself, and curl up like a dog. And the witch would run into the desert and find an anthill. Her clothes would be folded in a neat pile and her hair unbraided, loose upon her strong back, and she would roll in the ants, welcoming their small mouths. They would bite and bite and she would snap back.

Then she would become a coyote and sit on the hill, watching Mangwe Wakira, the weak man, a man without a woman.

One early morning when the sun was behind the mountains to the east, he built a fire and huddled around it, hands clasping his ankles, trying to get warm. It was a small fire, weak, with sticks the size of his fingers, and it sputtered and smoked. He shivered. He always felt eyes on him. He talked to himself. There were eyes on him, and tiny mouths, and something with a red breath came into his dreams when he was sleeping. When he was working in his fields, he often slept, his mouth slack, his arms moving back and forth, his breath slow as a squash petal unfurling. And the dreams were there then, too, the dreams of eyes on the back of his head, tiny eyes crawling up and down his body, and they were animal eyes and human eyes, and there was no difference between the two. A woman's eyes, he muttered to himself.

This morning the fire dried the wet dirt between his toes and the clumps of soil fell around him with soft hissing sounds. He wrapped his arms around his shoulders and shivered. He never thought much about life, except that it needed to be weeded and watered and that the moon meant something to plants and that the sun was hot and the night full of things that flew and gasped. He squatted in the dirt in front of the fire and didn't think.

Then he heard a strange voice. It wasn't the voice of the maize as it rustled in the wind or the voice of the water as he poured it from the cracked clay bowl onto the roots of the beans. Those were voices he understood.

He looked up.

"Sure is cold today, isn't it?" asked a coyote with a woman's eyes.

He jumped up and ran away, the seedlings on his cuffs falling out and shriveling in the cold air. He was never seen again.

Coyote Woman doesn't know why she did this. She didn't need a reason. She doesn't have to explain it to you. But it happened. All the women in my family remember her and know how it feels to pad softly under the moon, hunting things with weak bones, watching our men become frail as they sleep, like birds without wings.

Marking Time

Chronometry is the estimate, measurement, and record of time.
This is science.

Chronology is the determination of what happened when.
This is history.

Some events exist outside of historic time.
This is myth.

Some events become the memories of a people, a family, an individual.
This is a story.

The Esperanza Sisters

The Red-Hearted Desert

I am called Catalina.

Mi madre was una bruja, a powerful witch. The good kind of power that is given to you in the womb. She could fly night inside out and pace the edge of the unknown. She healed with herbs and had many lovers. One of them was mi padre, a poor man distinguished and enriched only by the fact that she desired him. Desire, she told me, is a map without boundaries, whereas love has its limits.

Brujas learn about borders, crossing the red-hearted desert under the bleached moon and feeling the stars' heat on the fur of their heads. The border between bodies and souls is like the ephemeral passageway from night to dawn.

In the old days, there was no chemical border between our ancient land and the one to the north: this was all one land. There were no factories offering our people the good life at forty-five centavos per day. We didn't drink well water that makes salt burn and boils rivers into acidic soups of curdled fish bones . . . we didn't have fingers that looked like small totems of death. *Ay*, we just had war and wounds where our eyes should be.

Mi madre taught me that the world was not always this way. In the old days, sticks grew in the desert with voices like the voices of old women. And there were giant scorpions and snakes, *sierpes*, who used to be people before they did bad things. In the old days, winds would come out of deep holes in the earth where the *sierpes* slept, dreaming of sucking small-breasted young girls and coiling around slim-waisted boys.

Dark-Blue Angel, Wet and Round

When I was born, I was already old. My mother was visiting her sister near Guaymas. They walked along the beach, looking for shells. My aunt lifted her small feet away from the advancing waves, but my mother stepped directly in the foam. She liked the way the sand sucked underfoot, as if the world was pulling itself out from under her.

A man pulled a boat up on the beach, then hurried away toward town, holding up a string of flat-sided fish, the tortilla fish, *taskai kuchu*, the one who told the little people, the Surem, that the sun was male just as it was.

Everyone was hungry then, some eating tree bark and rats. My mother became dizzy at the sight of the tortilla fish. So many children were dying. The parents gave their babies nicknames to fool the bad spirits, to keep the children safe. I rolled around inside my mother, tugging on the veined cord, elemental. Remembered when I'd lived in Tenochtitlán and the invaders set fire to the aviaries. My wings smoked, and in the updraft of flames, I flew to the top of the cage, where I was pressed into ashes and the wind scattered me in four directions.

While my aunt talked about her husband's big stomach, my mother waddled on, preoccupied with her own heavy stomach. She lifted her head. She could hear the sun painting her ears a rich coral color, each stroke of light brushing audibly. She could feel the earth positioning itself to the stars' circling. And then she heard the dolphins calling. Her water broke and fell back into the sea, streaming minerals of maize. A small eyelash of mine floated among the grains of sand.

In mid-sentence my aunt stopped chattering, halted, and turned around, her skirts dragging damply in the sand. She saw her sister kneeling in the water, a dolphin's head cradled on her lap. My mother stroked it gently while it sang a song, like a clicking moon. Then it slipped away and I was born, a little dark-blue angel, wet and round as a dolphin floundering in the hot sun. My mother breathed into me, her breath smelling like wet bamboo, and from a near distance, a drum beat pulsated into my own chest. Dusky pink, I cried, my voice like parched plants at the edge of rain.

Wild Canary

There is life beyond an instance, yet life adds up to a million such times. All the cells that combine to form my hair, tongue, fingers, heart do so in a song that differentiates itself only slightly from the song of a wild canary, the *sawali wiikit*. Yet my ear has heard the delicate tones and my eye has seen the flash of yellow and what once was *bird* now is cellular in my optic nerve and upon the small waxy hammer of the inner ear. I became a good singer, singing in the smoky cantinas and out in the desert, where the men like to drink around a mesquite fire. They sometimes said I was a bad woman, a *cantinera*, and maybe I was.

I've lived many lives. We are not just the sum of one existence. I've been young and stupid, young and proud. I've had a small waist and high-arched feet. I've had old breasts that flutter at every faltering heart beat. But I have not been just those things, those physical things. I am the ancient spells, the fire, the harsh words that flay skin, the slow beauty of every first morning. I am Coyote Woman. I am La Morena, the Dark One. I am . . . the first rule that all birds must circle the earth over bones, stones, and salt.

Now that I'm old, I try to keep one foot in the ocean at all times, especially when I'm dreaming. If you dream deep enough, the dolphins will circle back to their beginnings, away from the nets of poison. Now that I'm old, when my heart skips a beat I can hear the sea rushing into my ears, ready to pull me back into its song.

Fish Heads

That's not the way it happened. When you tell a story, you should get it right. That is, let *me* tell it.

My name is Concepción, but I have no children. I was the pretty one. My sister Gloria, who gave birth on the beach, was *la sabia*, the wise one. There were some who called her worse. Said she was *la bruja* and knew how to twist men's guts up under their tongues until they were panting for her. She has a broad nose and full lips; not beautiful, said the Sisters of Josephine. But she had a knowing look in her eye that made all the men look twice.

When my sister came out of the mountains to visit me, she was pregnant. She wrapped her head in a black shawl and kept her eyes on her belly. It was the safest way to be a woman, unless you were like me: married to a Mexican. Some of my family won't speak to me, but Arturo is a good man. My sister laughs when I call him El Gordo, the fat one.

He believes a man's girth reflects his importance. He has often been mistaken for the priest, but El Gordo can walk a straight line. Drink isn't one of his weaknesses. Only food. When times were prosperous, I dedicated myself to creating a man of great stature, a man with a stomach the size of his soul.

But now food is scarce. Arturo's stomach boomed, snapped, and popped so loudly that the dog ran away, thinking the federales were shooting Yaquis again. I yelled at Arturo bitterly. That dog was our next meal.

I told my sister about the tomato plants. The fruit was withering. The chilies were like shriveled dark penises. I covered my face suddenly. I shouldn't have talked about such things when she was carrying a child.

We watched a fisherman. His boat grated against the sand as he drew it up on the beach. We could hear the rasp of his knife against the shining scales of the fish as he cut off the heads. We held out our skirts and the man gave us fish heads, the eyes staring coldly at us like nuns.

Skull to Crown

Three dolphins jumped out into the sky. I closed my eyes, sick with hunger, imagining the dolphins cut up into chunks of sweet meat, floating in a sauce of tomatoes and cilantro.

Then Gloria fell to her knees. I helped her to the shade of a palm tree, the brown fronds littering the beach. I knelt in front of her open thighs, the dark folds of her skin flushed with blood, straining white. I waited for the baby's skull to crown, waited for another skeleton to be born.

She screamed and pushed. Shivered. Clenched fistfuls of sand. Gloria had been hiding in the mountains for almost a year now, with the other Yaquis, ever since the federales started rounding us up and sending many to Yucatán. I could see how she'd changed, becoming more mountain herself, with the slope of her belly and the hard ridges of her shoulders.

I wanted the baby to never know hunger. I held out my hands, which smelled of the memory of fresh tortillas, sweet corn, fiery chilies the shape of my Gordo's nose. My fingers smelled like watermelon and crushed cumin, like water spiced with cinnamon, and the long cool dreams of green bean pods. The baby came out with her mouth open, and I let her suck on my fingers until they were bones.

Teresa

I knew she would be a girl. We are a family of powerful women, with eyes the far side of coyote's moon. One sister, Teresa, was educated by the Sisters of Josephine at Bacum, who believed that someday a great revolutionary would come and bring equality for women and Yaquis. They gave her a cross and a gun. They filled her head with dreams of strong-muscled women and clean clothes, fat-cheeked babies, and men who gave courtly bows whenever they requested a dance.

She cut off her hair and rode to the mountains with a handsome Yaqui. They say that later she gave birth to a baby, biting bullets to keep herself quiet during labor, then spitting them out again, killing ten Mexican soldiers. She asked Gloria, sister-witch, to make a *choni*. It's a small piece of an Apache's scalp, the long hair tied with a red ribbon. Teresa commanded it to find the Mexican soldier who raped our youngest sister, Cruz. Very early one morning, the choni found him, snoring under a bush near Hermosillo. The choni floated through the air, wrapped its long hair three times around the soldier's neck, and choked him to death. His bulging eyes looked like the eyes of a dead tortilla fish.

A Butterfly with the Eyes of a Woman

Another sister, Dominga, followed an American scientist and his bag of pins. With a net, he chased a cloud of black and orange butterflies. We never saw her again, although we heard a strange story about a curiosity shop in Durango that had the world's largest butterfly pinned to a board. It had the eyes of a woman. The pin went straight through the heart.

Gloria tells it differently, of course. She says that hunger is stronger than love. Our butterfly sister shrank to the bones while her stomach swelled up like a cocoon. When the sky fluttered with butterflies bringing rain, her soul fled west with them.

Lead Rosary

And Teresa wasn't a great revolutionary, living in the mountains with her man, his gun between her legs. She was only a woman fighting for life, carrying her baby on her back wrapped in a dirty blanket, riding a sweating horse until her legs were rubbed raw. Later, she went back to the nuns and sent them to hell with a rosary of lead bullets.

Cruz was deported to Yucatán. One day they ordered her to Guaymas, where she was packed on a small boat. She carried her baby wrapped up in her rebozo and cradled his tiny head with one hand. In San Blas, she was shoved off the boat along with many other women. From there, she was force-marched to another town. On the third day, her son died. The federales took away his tiny body with an old man's face. We heard about this from Victoria García, who later returned to Hermosillo, but we never saw Cruz again. Victoria thought Cruz died, worked to death on the hemp plantations.

The Only Story

My life is not heroic. I take in washing for the Mexican soldiers, hurrying out of the way of their boots. I watch them laugh at my Gordo. They call him Stink Bug. His stomach is thin as a rat's tail. He hunches in his shadow, teeth like dried corn rattling in his mouth, his eyes looking back at a time when he was respected, a grand man. I love him because he suffers with me when he could cast me off and take a Mexican woman for a wife.

I suck the food stains on the soldier's clothing. I watch the rough-ribbed dogs standing motionless by the old people. I see the dogs waiting for their bones.

And so, into such a world of hunger, a baby is born. A baby called Catalina falls into my hands, falling into her own story. And I remember we are all storytellers. We are living the hunger of the soul for life.

And this is true. Each of us is thinking: *My own story is the only one worth living*.

Honey

The wind walked out of the rocks. We heard the earth talking, the deep hearts of the mountains beating slowly. Here there is a story that is many stories. The mountains know all about us.

The wind walked in a changing way. First, wind was a long-legged animal with sand swirling in its belly. Then wind stood up like a bear, clawing at us. Finally, it slithered away around a boulder, hissing and gliding.

We climbed higher, looking for honey.

Father stopped, wiped his forehead. "The sky is darkening."

My brother and I could see only a fine blueness. We looked at each other. Maybe Father was seeing a different sky, one like a garden of dark flowers. We know there is a place called *sea ania*, the flower world, where it is good and beautiful. Father has a special power. It is called *seataka*. It tells him many things and he isn't afraid of it, even though it sometimes makes him fly in his dreams.

My little brother shook his head. He's too young to understand. He took my hand.

Then Father said, "Listen! Can you hear the bees?"

I turned my ear up. There was a noise like my finger rubbing on one of my hairs pulled tight. A high sound. But not the sound of bees. It was only the mountain singing.

We climbed higher, following an ancient path. Father rubbed his arm.

"The bees are stinging me!"

My brother and I laughed. Father looked funny slapping at his arm. He must know what will happen. I can almost taste the sweet honey in my mouth. I like chewing on the combs, too.

This morning when we got up, Father said that he'd dreamt about Yomumuli. She told him where to find a honey tree. Now, he shook his arm and peered ahead.

I think I'll see the tree first, but my brother says, no, *he* will. I want to find a tree made of bees and flowers, of pollen and sky. All around us is the flower-covered wilderness and our little deer brothers, the red quail with their topknots, *bisa*, and above us, sometimes you can see a comet, with its fiery headdress, a star headdress, *choki bisa*. It's all here if you look. Father taught us to look.

Now I see a *taka sevo'i*, a heaven fly. It is flying down from a branch of the sky and I'm afraid. When you see a heaven fly, it means something bad will happen.

"Father," I start to say, but he falls down. His ear is pressed to the earth. What is he listening for?

Maybe he hears the water that breathes inside the mountains or the roots of bamboo, *vakateteve*.

But when I get down to the ground I see Father's eyes rolling in the sockets like quail eggs. Grabbing his shoulders, I tug until he turns over. His mouth is opening and closing, his lips fluttering like wings. Humming comes from his chest, like a hive of bees, a storm of bees. I hold him and his eyes stay open all day. What he sees is his spirit, *hiapsi*, flying away.

Little brother cries.

Together we pull Father's arms, we tumble him over and over, until we push him into a small indentation of the mountain. I can hear Omteme shouting at Columbus, there in the mountain. I can hear arrows splitting Father's heart in half. We cover him with rocks. It takes a long time, and when we're done, we're very tired. Little brother is still sniffling.

We feel small like ants. When Father was alive he was between us and everything big: the sky, the soldiers, hunger. Now I'm suddenly smaller than I was this morning. Little brother has his thumb in his mouth. I must decide what to do next. Our shadows are growing away from us. We eat the dried corn in our pouches, drink from the gourd. Little brother wants to go home. But I think: we don't have Father and we don't have honey. If we go back now, we have nothing but bad news. If we get the honey, Mother will be pleased. So now I make a big decision: we'll go after the honey. I feel a little older, but little brother's face is puckered up. He won't look at me. He wants to know if the little ant people will show our Father the way home. Sí, I whisper, and he nods, eyes searching for our ant cousins.

He steps carefully as we climb. Yes, we're climbing higher, listening for the humming noise at the top of the world.

Note: My great-grandfather Valentino went hunting for honey with his father in the Bacatete Mountains. His father died up there, and Valentino and his brother had to bury him.

Estefana's Necklace of Bullets

Pack trains traveled from Yaqui country to the port of Guaymas, carrying goods such as salt, guns and gunpowder, textiles, metal tools, parakeets, lard, and sugar.

"They were Mexicans dressed like Indians," said the man. He had a strong voice and his wide hat shadowed his face. It was possible that he wore a mask defined by the concentration camps of the silver mines. It was likely he wore his eyes like the eyes in a Picasso painting. It was probable that he'd lost one hand somewhere near a soldier's sword. Maybe he didn't even miss his hand. You can do a lot with what's left when you think everything's been taken away from you.

He had a good voice. So he carried the news from town to town.

The man repeated his message patiently to the woman. She stood still, one hand on the door frame, mouth open. When she didn't faint, and he didn't expect her to, he continued.

"They killed Pedro. Took all his money, goods, and burros."

She chewed her lip, then brushed him aside. She was a tiny woman, only four feet, eleven inches. On her hips were two large pistols. A bandoleer of bullets was draped across her chest. Before she answered her door, she always put on her guns and necklace of bullets.

He watched her stride away toward the village *capitán*. He strolled after her, feeling his phantom hand pouring lead into bullet molds, then handing the hardened bullets to her. His phantom hand unpinned her hair. His phantom hand lifted her skirts . . .

At the sound of her pounding on the capitán's door, the messenger was jerked out of his daydream. He looked down at his remaining hand. He wanted to keep it. He knew if he touched her, this woman would chew off his other hand. Everyone knew she had a bad temper. Still, she was beautiful.

The capitán opened the door.

"¡Señora!"

"Mi esposo, my husband, is dead. He's been murdered." She related what little she knew and then looked over her shoulder for the messenger, but he was gone. "You must find who killed him."

The capitán smoothed his mustache. "I don't know enough. How will I find who killed him? There're bandits everywhere."

He blinked at her. He'd been sleeping. Estefana Garica Ramos whirled around him, brandishing her pistols. He saw a swirl of long black hair and lots of teeth. A beautiful demon. He took a deep breath.

"Did you hear me?" She glared at him. He nodded and pretended to think about the problem.

So her husband, the trader and smuggler Pedro, was dead, was he? Often he had suspected Pedro of supplying goods, guns, and ammunition to the Yaqui rebels hiding in the mountains. But he hadn't known for sure.

He'd heard Pedro had given his daughter a gold slipper. Carlotta was also lovely and well educated by the nuns. She could even read and write in Spanish, which the capitán couldn't. He was illiterate. He couldn't figure out how Pedro could be so rich if he was just a simple peddler. Lessons from the nuns cost money, too.

But for all her education, Estefana needed his help. He liked the feeling. Standing up straighter, he told her he'd do what he could.

She shook her head and lifted the guns to his chest. He remembered then another story he'd heard. She had been at the man who pulls teeth when he pulled the wrong one out! She chased the man through the streets, shooting at him.

He felt his knees grow weak.

"You!" she said. "If you don't find who killed my husband, you'll be the next to die."

Sidling past her, he hurried away, glancing back once. She still held the guns on him. He broke into a run.

Note: This story is told about my great-grandmother Estefana. I don't know whether the capitán ever found out who killed my great-grandfather, or even exactly when it happened; it could have been as late as 1905. None of Pedro's wealth was recovered.

An interesting mystery arises about the "gold slipper." What was it exactly? After hearing the family story, I puzzled over the fact that it was only one gold slipper. Was it a gold-colored shoe, its mate lost? Was it a charm for a necklace or bracelet? Family members insisted it was real gold. No one knew what had become of it, and I couldn't figure it out.

Then, while researching this book, I read *Tall Candle*, a memoir by the Yaqui Rosalio Moisés (1896–1969). One day, at Hermosillo in Sonora, Moisés visited a house at La Playita orchard. The owner of the house was out for the day, so Jesús Álvarez, the groundskeeper and a friend of Moisés, let him in. Moisés remembered that he walked around, trying not to touch anything. His friend Jesús warned him to keep his hands in his pockets, but Moisés couldn't help himself. He saw a tiny gold pincushion shaped like a shoe. Since his father had been a gold miner, Moisés was positive it was real gold. He took it.

After the owners returned, doña Concha realized her pincushion was gone. When she questioned the groundskeeper, Jesús told her he hadn't taken it, not knowing that his friend Moisés had. When the news got around about the missing gold shoe, Moisés threw it away in a field.

I wonder if my great-grandfather Pedro Ramos found the gold shoe and gave it to his daughter to use as a pincushion.

Bones Resembling My Grandfather

SONORA, MEXICO, 1889–1937

I hid behind the porch made of sticks. The sticks were like a row of starving men without any heads. The stick men were so hungry that nothing was left of them but crooked ribs. Yet they hid me, their little bone brother.

My grandfather had many names: Meetah, Emery, Emiteria.

When the soldiers came, my father, Valentino, told me to hide.

His last name was Diaz, after the dictator of Mexico.

I saw them tie his hands and then kick him. They cut him, shot him, killed him in a thousand ways . . .

. . . their Mexican-Nazi boots stomping his eyes into the ground until the whole world soon saw swastikas like dirty stars

falling

blinding everyone.
But not
      La Morena
the Dark One, Mother of the Eater of Filth, who looks like a skull today. Fashionable dead-white lipstick, eyes deep holes corpses fall into, mouth slack-jawed, teeth rattling around in my pocket. She's laughing at me, at my hunger for life. I'm telling you my grandfather's story and she thinks it's funny that we are shocked by so much death. La vida es la muerte. She grins, licks her necklace of human hearts.

She interferes with the telling, this woman, this Hungry Woman, who is somehow related to me in all these stories and who promises that death is also a gentle novia, lover.

I am so hungry. But I'm Yaqui and strong. I'm leaving this place, walking north to los Estados Unidos, where I'll be safe from the soldiers. I won't be afraid anymore.

Okay, so my grandfather Meetah didn't know about Wounded Knee or Custer or Kit Carson. Meetah was just a boy. A boy who saw his father murdered and still believed Earth could be a good place.

I'll follow the railroad tracks. Not south to Yucatán where they've deported so many Yaquis to slave labor on the hemp plantations.

Cattle cars packed with people. Sounds familiar, doesn't it, Hungry Woman? Who said that the world practiced genocide first on this continent, then when they got it down pat they started killing Jews and other undesirables?

I'll go north. To the Salton Sea.

Meetah scooped up handfuls of mud and made a turban of wet earth on his head to keep away sunstroke. His pale skin, with a natural reddish tint, darkened and blistered.

I'll find a place where ohvo, blood, doesn't scream from the earth, where the earth has no hungry mouths, where I can wear my bones inside my flesh. I'll make it. I'm almost a man. I can ride horses and shoot straight. No bloody skulls and chopped-off hands will ever touch me.

My father said Meetah was five feet eleven inches tall and weighed 210 pounds. He could lift 400 pounds easily. He was stocky. An excellent marksman with both handgun and rifle, he fought both whites and Mexicans if he had to. "He was always ready for trouble," said my father, "and he lived his life like other Indians. He didn't like Mexicans." He rode all over the Southwest, training horses.

All the ladies like me. The white women especially like the way I sing, but the Mexican señoritas are afraid of me.

He was a good dancer, too. "He had many friends, both Indian and white," remembered my father. He played the Jew's harp and the harmonica.

But there are the dreams. Soldiers. Death is a bayonet with my father's heart on it.
No matter how far I ride, the dreams follow me. I drink only to forget what should never be forgotten.

Then he went to L.A., where helicopters now hover like mechanical angels with one single bright eye and homeboys run down alleys casting swastika shadows on the white stucco walls. But in those days, in the early 1920s, there were bean fields and orange groves and roots were not bones in the soil. The shadows were only citrus-scented leaves, not dark hands nailed to the sky.

I pick prunes, apricots, walnuts with my children. A man should keep his word, to himself and others. A man should protect his children, love his wife, that woman who feeds those poorer than we are, out of the goodness of her heart. A man should be happy with his friends . . . but I'm not a man in my bones. My heart is a rag bundle; my soul like a horse broken with stones, not kind words. Every night, Carlotta sings to me or plays the nine-string guitar with her long fingers. Still, I can hear my father's last breath, and my throat rattles until más cervezas float my heart into the gentle hands of La Morenita.

On September 19, 1937, Meetah was killed in Long Beach, California, a few blocks from his junkyard business (and his home) by a hit-and-run driver. They say his normally black hair turned gray when he died. The autopsy reported that he had skull fractures, a punctured lung, a collapsed lung, and broken bones. He was probably drunk.

Grandfather Sun Falls in Love
with a Moon-Faced Woman

He was probably drunk, you know, on maize mixed with water. That night, that night, he fell in love for the first time of this life. It was not the first time he drank to forget the long journey, the tramping through alkaline dust white as ground bones, the mud packed on his head like a beehive. It was not the first time he drank to remember the feel of wild horses between his legs and how they would sigh in the morning.

She had a cool, silvery light in her face, the way a woman looks when she bends over still water and studies her face. Or the way water flickers in sea caves, that bending of light and water, sleek as a seal. She was his opposite in many ways: patient when he was hotheaded, quiet when he shouted in anger at life, the cords of his neck strong as bullwhips.

When he approached her, she lifted her chin and stared at him. "You've been watching me," she stated.

"Will you marry me?" he asked. "Will you marry me?" He sat down abruptly, weakened by his boldness.

She laughed. "You're funny."

When he hung his head, shoulders sloping down into his pockets, she laughed harder. "Oh, I like a man who makes me laugh!"

He looked up and grinned. Maybe this was going to turn out all right.

"You men!" she scolded, her face shining in the dark edge of dawn. The strap of her red dress slid down one shoulder. She canted one hip, angling her ankle until the high-heeled shoe slipped off and the small space between heel and earth was like red earth and roses.

He wanted to kiss her heels, let her walk across him, the way he walked across Sonora. Let her step into him, to what he'd become, sitting here on the seawall listening to the Pacific Ocean call her name.

Over and over, he smiled, wanting to make her laugh again. He bared his teeth, pulled his upper lip to cover his nose, let his lips hang loose while he warbled Mexican love songs. She laughed so hard, she grabbed her middle and bent over into the ocean.

"Okay," she gasped, "I'll marry you . . . on one condition."

He sat up suddenly. "¿Qué?" But she was already gone.

The next night he got there early, said ¡Hola! to the last of the evening's sea-gulls, who screamed at him.

Well, let them, he thought. He waited for her to stroll down the street again, wearing that dress the color of ripe peaches. He had picked peaches all day, took his money, letting the jingle of coins remind him of spurs. He used to break horses in Arizona, riding the sweat-sleek mustangs until they stopped, quivering, accept-ing the bit and the hard hawing of his hands on the reins. Now, he was reduced to twisting peaches from their branches, stepping in the rotten flesh, swatting at hor-nets. Peaches or walnuts, strawberries or lettuce. He'd gone one step lower on the chain of dominance. From animal to vegetable.

I'm a vegetable, he swore to himself, as he tipped back the bottle. He hiccuped. I'm a pickled vegetable. He chuckled softly.

"What's so funny?" she asked. This time she looked a little different, but you know how women can change themselves. It's in their makeup.

But he didn't feel funny after all. He felt sad. Maybe a little bit angry. Okay, a lot angry, if you want to know the truth. He had walked all the way from Mexico in order to end up a vegetable in a country that thought he was scum because he was an Indian.

She sat down beside him. Her skirt was real short and he smelled her, the corn-flower smell of her thighs. "Doncha wanna get hitched?" she asked in a low, teasing voice.

He tried to sit up straighter, but vegetables have roots, and his spine was at-taching itself to the cement seawall. He was about to become a mineral if he didn't rouse himself.

"Sí." He glanced at her. She made him nervous. She wore a white dress, just like a bride. No veil. No Bible. Did she mean now, like get married *now*?

"Remember?" she asked, staring intently at him.

He was stuck. Remember what? He narrowed his eyes, trying to read the dark-ness. Somewhere there was an answer. He licked his finger and placed it on an imaginary page, turning it, hoping for answers to fly out at him like pale doves.

"You don't remember, do you?!" She stood up, narrow and suddenly slender, like a sword. "¡Ay, men!" She turned away from him, standing stiffly.

He sweated. Small drops of fermented maize gathered on his brow. I'm sweat-ing vegetables, he thought. He shook his head, flinging off tiny corn plants twisted into the shapes of drunken men.

"Okay, okay," he mumbled, not looking at her. "What did I forget?"

She sighed. It was *that* sigh, the one women make when they think their men have brains like dried calabashes.

"I said I'd marry you." She paused. "On one condition."

"What's that?"

She sat down next to him, the white dress floating like waves around her knees. "You must bring me a gift that will fit me precisely."

He nodded, tried to coax a smile from her by holding his lips inside his mouth until he looked like an old man. But she didn't smile, and he felt foolish. She was too beautiful to be reminded that someday he would be an old man. Maybe he was already.

"At least I have my teeth," he said and was horrified to realize he'd spoken aloud. But when he turned to look at her she was gone, and he thought he saw her thin light glowing on the barnacle-encrusted pier.

The next day he bought only a little corn whiskey. Just enough to loosen his muscles, let the bones straighten out from a day of carrying canvas bags of peaches slung over one shoulder, each bag heavy as a body. One bag over each shoulder, the peaches hard as baby skulls, punching his back. With the other money, the money left over from not buying so much whiskey, he bought her a gift.

All day he had thought about what he should get her, but he couldn't afford any of those things. A peach tree, a garden, a field, a house, a village, the whole city. A city of angels, los angeles, lace mantillas, a gold avocado.

He bought her a belt from Woolworth's. It was white and would go with that white dress. Women liked things that matched, he knew. It might even look good with the red dress. It was a shiny patent leather belt, with a gold-colored buckle and three tiny gold eyelets for the clasp. He wrapped it in the sack the whiskey came in and tied it with a string he'd stolen from the peach bags.

He walked down the pier, whistling. It was an old Yaqui song somebody had taught him long ago. Or maybe didn't teach him, he just remembered it. After his father was killed by the soldiers, no one taught him anything anymore. He was through with learning. All he wanted was to get away. The only thing that was important was that he was alive. Nothing else mattered.

Now, suddenly, when he was a man, love mattered. How it had happened, how he had fallen in love with her, he didn't know. He never knew those kinds of things. He knew how to make music from his mouth and how to calm a horse, lifting its leg in order to clean the hoof. He knew how to eat strawberries without moving his mouth so that the boss wouldn't say he was stealing while he worked. He knew how to sleep under a bench in a park. He knew how to forget where he was. *That* was important. Why did the fathers never teach you things like that?

She sauntered up. This time she was wearing a yellow sarong, like you see in the movie posters, that Hollywood lady. Her breasts were pushed up, two golden moons. He took a deep breath and offered the package to her.

"¡Ay!" she exclaimed. Like a child, she tore at the wrapping, but stopped to look at him. She smiled shyly. Then she continued, unfolding the package. The white belt lay coiled like a ghost snake, a moon snake with gold head and three gold eyes. She put it around her waist.

Even he could see it was too big. It looked like a barrel hoop. She shook her head as the belt fell to her feet. Her waist was so slender he could see the lean shadows of palm-leaf ribs fluttering through her. She was so thin she was almost transparent.

As she walked away, she looked over her shoulder. "Mañana."

The next day he bought her a bracelet, small enough for a child, made out of a pretty blue plastic. He spat on it, shining it up with the edge of his shirt, then wrapped it a page of the L.A. *Times*.

He found his spot on the seawall. Took the bottle from his pocket and tipped it until he saw her face glowing in the other end. Quickly, he stopped drinking, wiping his mouth with the back of his hand. He handed her the gift.

She took the bracelet from the sports page and tried to slip it over her hand, but it wouldn't work. The bracelet was too small.

"You got big hands," he said, wondering if that was okay to say to a woman. They didn't like you talking about their big feet or noses. She was looking at him in a strange way. Smiling a bit. But looking as if he wasn't there or she wasn't seeing him. She shook her head, long hair flowing around her, down to her waist.

She looked more substantial today, he decided. A little heavier, maybe. He cocked his head, watching her as she sashayed away, buttocks bouncing like plump peaches. Well, he told himself, don't women get that way. Something to do with the time of the month.

The following day he gave her nothing. It was raining so hard his liquor got diluted, even though he tried to save it by swallowing fast. The next night it was foggy, and he looked for her. She never showed up. Two nights later, the fog blew away and he saw her, strolling down the beach. She looked fat. Just a little, but nice, you know, like you knew you'd find a lot of woman under the ivory-colored caftan. Big round breasts, like melons, and a stomach round as a tomato. A vegetable woman for a vegetable man. He liked that.

But she didn't like his gift. It was a scarf, yellow with white butterflies. It was supposed to fit across her shoulders but was so dwarfed by her greatness that she could have used it as a hankie for her nose. She shook her head and left him.

Bad weather again. No work in the fields, either. No money. No gift. He stood around the alley, sharing a bottle with Rubio and some other mouths.

"Hey, man," sneered one, "ain't this the life?"

"Don't fuck with me," said Rubio. Water dripped off his hair. He looked like a wet chihuahua, shivering in the rain. He took another drink, passed the bottle to another mouth.

"Not fuckin' with you, man. Just talkin', ya know, makin' conversation."

"Well, shuddup."

The rain sounded like drums. Powwow drums. There were drums up in the hills overlooking L.A., singers, too. Mostly displaced Sioux, some of them sent to California to learn how to become civilized, others hoping for a job acting in the movies. He'd gone up once, wanting to be with other Indians who knew they were Indians, as opposed to all those Indians who thought they were Mexicans. He'd gone up to hear the drums and stayed all night, feeling the soft beating coming out of the men's hearts, into their arms, into the drums, then out into the earth, the night air, and into him. When they asked who he was, he said, "I'm Yaqui," and they nodded.

Later they called him Sun because his skin got hot when he drank, sweat sizzling off his cheeks. When the sun came up, he rode back to town with them, six Indians in the back of a pickup, rattling down the switchbacks, tires swaybacked and lame.

He must've fallen in love up there, he thought. That's when it happened. Before he even saw her, he knew he was going to fall in love. It must've been the singing or the drums shaking his dick, rumbling around in his balls until his whole body hummed with wanting.

And he wanted her, waited for the rain to stop, so he could see her again. Drank some more, hoping it was a kind of magic, making a liquid go inside of him so that liquid falling outside would stop. Any dumb thing, to make her come back. Her bright face, round shoulders, fleshy knees.

So when the rain did stop, he wasn't dried out enough to make it over to the seawall. He missed one night. Couldn't remember it going like that. A night that hadn't happened. Sometimes time was that way. But he made it back there the following night and brought her a tablecloth he swiped from someone's backyard on

Rio Street. It was a white tablecloth with wine stains on it, but he thought they were pale roses. He had a headache and his eyes hurt.

When she strutted up, he was shocked. She was thin, like a cocktail stirrer. Wore a black dress and spiked heels. Some kind of glassy black rocks for earrings. Her eyes were enormous.

She held up the tablecloth, which he hadn't wrapped at all. A question in her eyes.

"It's a cape," he suggested frantically, "like the rich ladies wear."

She wrapped it around her shoulders. Once, twice, three times she wrapped herself, until she stood like a cocoon and the ancient word for butterfly came fluttering back to him from a past in another land. *Vaeseuoli.*

The tablecloth unwound itself from her thin body. It fell, full of wine and roses and gravy, puddling around her feet. Her ankles were thin as icepicks. She had no hips, just two sharp plates of bone. Her belly was an empty cup. Her breasts were only nipples, two suggestions.

"This isn't going to work," she said sadly. "Nothing fits me precisely."

He stared at his hands. *They* would fit her, mold her, precisely. And his mouth could fit hers. If she'd only give him a chance . . . he'd be a good lover.

"Sorry," she said. Again she made him nervous. And suddenly, he knew why: she had no purse. Other women carried purses, fiddled with them while they flirted, pulled out tubes of red and magenta lipstick, round puffs for powder, little circles of mirrors that gave them his point of view of their lips. Keys, coins, mad money, taxi money, coffee money.

But she had no purse. As if she never needed redder lips or pots of rouge, small bottles of perfume. Or as if she was complete in herself, like a man, not needing a purse to hold in front of her like a shield. Such confidence was unnerving. Real women needed men. He wanted her to need him.

And she didn't. She walked away, narrow as a bone, dark hair braided into one sparse thread. She never looked back.

But he kept looking at her. Every night. He fell.
He fell in love.
He fell in love with her.
He fell.

He drank and fell
down, looking for her at the bottom of the bottle.
Those eyes, those lips.

He got married. To an ordinary, beautiful Yaqui woman. One who was smart with money. And who took care of him and the children. A really good woman, with another child born before his. Angelita. A little angel. Not his wife's fault she was raped, but she loved the girl. His wife even loved tramps, gave them food when they knocked on the back door. Tortillas wrapped around stewed chicken. Clear, cold water from the tap. A song from her heart.

Sí, so he was married. But he never stopped mooning for *her*.

When the car came out of the night, he was Sun, hot and feeling the blood pounding in his feet. He danced in the street, watching the headlights give him a stage. He bent over, waiting for the applause, bottle in one hand. It was a magic bottle, like the kind in the stories from Arabia, where a tiny spirit lived inside and gave you whatever you wished. He kept her there and drank until he got what he wanted.

It took a long time to figure out what that was.

So when the car hit him, he thought it was love again. A big punch to the solar plexus.

A real jab to the heart.

He rolled to the side of the street. The car roared away. He laughed when he saw the bottle was unbroken and the moon jangled around inside it, in her white wedding dress. She laughed, too. Good joke.

Knew what he could give her. Should've known then, long ago. What fit, what fit perfectly. Now it was there: in his heart. A package wrapped in blood red. He opened his hand; the bottle fell, clinking.

The gift that fits: one size fits all. *Amor. Love.*

She smiled.

He stirred the stars with his fingers, watched the fragments of light splinter the darkness. Saw her, full and round and womanly. He lay with his head on her lap. He lay with his head on the curb.

Note: The preceding story is a modern version of an old Yaqui myth about the sun and the moon and recounts the waxing and waning of the moon. And love. Or maybe it's about my grandfather Emiterio, who was killed in a hit-and-run accident in 1937.

The Esperanza Sisters, Continued

Vow

Yo soy Cruz. I was born in Sonora, Mexico, and will die in Long Beach, California, at age ninety-nine. When I was fifteen, I was sent to the hemp plantation. I carried my little son wrapped in a rebozo, but he died and the soldiers took him away. I think they fed him to the dogs.

My son's father was a good man. He was shot by the federales.

I worked hard in the fields of Yucatán. I was a slave but not without my freedom to suffer. After my fourth child died, I placed her in the heart of a maguey plant where the sharp spines pierced her skin, and I let the skull-skirted Aztec woman take her into the Peninsula of Darkness. (My children had different fathers: the overseer, a Chinese laundryman, and a man who took me among the coiled hemp ropes. I went willingly only to the laundryman because he looked a bit like my cousin Alfonso Delgado. You may have heard of him. He was well known for eating only maize; indeed, he dressed himself in maize leaves and wove sandals from the plant fibers. Later, he developed a bad disease of the skin and thereafter ate only shrimp and chilies. He was a dedicated man, like my Chinese husband, who scrubbed clothes with his bare knuckles.)

The night she died, she with her small blue fingers, unnamed and curled like a little mouse, I cried, wandering into the ruins of pyramids where once the sun and the moon were exactly enthroned on stone calendars. I wept without tears, my breasts engorged with milk and aching. When I saw the man by the well, eating his supper of beans and coffee, I cut off his head with his own machete. Everyone has her own way of mourning. I ate his food, wiped my mouth on his hair, and threw his head into the *cenote*, the well.

Then I looked at the Mexicano stars and followed their shadows in the dust of a long road. I ran away, away until I found a drunk man with crossed eyes. Because of this, he tended to walk in circles. I helped him by banging the side of his head with a cooking pot. One eye wobbled, then focused correctly, but the other eye always looked in the bottle.

We neglected our pasts, crossed the river to El Norte, entered the desert, where the sun is shredded on flint-sharp mountains and the desiccated moon never rises above sea level. The man, José Cabeza de Hoofer y de Heifer, descendant of the famous lost-white-man-who-could-not-read-maps, Cabeza de Vaca, headed off into the desert one day before I awoke at our campsite. I followed his fumes until I found a small pile of ashes shaped like a cow patty. Spontaneous combustion, I thought, fueled by alcohol and the hot sun. There was no mourning for him, although we had prayed together, wore each other's smell for a little while, riding the same horse of hunger.

I kept walking. I'm the history of the Esperanza women. We all keep walking, our skins female by proximity to our hearts. Even in the barrenness of shimmering desert, we see our reflections in the mirage. We follow the watery illusions of birth, remembering that our name means "hope." It is why we never give up, even in East L.A., where I finally knelt to drink deeply of the running waters in the gutters and where my grandson died in a drive-by shooting in Boyle Heights, his blood flowing down those same gutters. I wear my name on my bent back.

We all have a vow to life, to live. We follow our own roads, or make the road-less deserts our own journeys. The path behind us is only one way we could have gone. Somewhere, my dead children climb hemp ropes, dreaming about what is unraveled, those broken stars. Somewhere, the headless man loves his mother and closes his beautiful eyes against the watery goddess dancing in the limestone well. Somewhere, gravity keeps me from flying away, away, and not these heavy sandals, with their thick tire soles and hemp straps.

Now my great-granddaughter drinks sparkling water from water boutiques, she with her strong white fluoride teeth and dark *india* eyebrows. She's never lost, unlike her white-men ancestors; she rollerblades through Long Beach with her chili-pepper spray and long legs. Doves fly around her as she eats up the miles, vacationing in Acapulco, Mazatlán, Yucatán.

"Abuelita," she writes home on a postcard, "yesterday we saw the pyramids, the Chiapas T-shirt and bumper sticker store. Today we did the hemp plantations. It was just like you said, hot. We're going out dancing tonight. The people are poor here, but happy. I'd like to live here because everything is sooo cheap. Don't worry, I'm not drinking the tap water. Wish you were here, love, me."

Angelina

No one talks about her: Angelina. Her name sounds pretty, like the gold
    gilt-edged statues with wings and rouged cheeks I see at mass. Angelina.

She didn't look like my father or the rest of them: Johnny, Kuti, Pilar. Kiko.
    But she was my grandmother Carlotta's child: blue-eyed, blonde
    Angelina.

Not a miraculous conception, life embedded spiritually in Carlotta's womb,
not that, not that.

Carlotta was raped by Mexican soldiers, back when Yaqui hands were cut
    off and nailed
Christ-like to boards, rows of hands, palms out, fingers curled slightly

so that you can see the nails hammered through the palms and the ragged
    edges

of the wrists. So you can see all the hands that once smoothed a baby's hair

and patted tortillas and dug, broken nailed, into the earth for *plata*. Quotas
of silver, and if there wasn't enough, then you were truly empty-handed.

But Carlotta kept her hands. And her baby. Angelina, child born under the
    severed
stars of the Mexican Revolution, small angel wrapped in shawls,

named *Angelina* because her mother refused
to let evil win. Later, Dad says no one talks to Angelina anymore,

ever since she wouldn't accept five one-dollar bills
when my father tried to pay her back the five-dollar bill

he had borrowed in 1942 to buy my brother medicine.
This was forty years ago. And when I ask about Angelina

no one remembers her, or will tell me why they have a blue-eyed sister,
or why she held them in such enmity, or was it just contrariness,

or where she is buried with her hands folded loosely
so that anywhere I walk I may be walking on an angel,

knowing that the heart of an angel can become friable,
easily crushed by the boots of this world.

La Morena as the Sad-Eyed Jaguar Priest

It's better to be alive. When Dad got sent home from the navy, he laid out his medals on the kitchen counter: a spatula for flipping the shit they gave him and a can opener that he had tried to use on the bow of the ship the night he left. He thought he could peel the ship open like a tin of sardines and let his life fall out into the sea off of San Diego. But he was so deranged he forgot he was a descendant of desert Indians and couldn't swim.

He was so deranged that when they pulled him out of the waves, he *thanked* them. They gave him a piece of paper: a treaty between him and the government. He was honorably discharged into the rest of his life. He folded the paper carefully into a square animal that had yellow eyes and the soul of a jaguar priest.

Dad wasn't a warrior, though. The only things he ever fought were TB and his wives. He was a cook in the navy until he hurt his back lifting pounds of potatoes. After his discharge he got married. She worked in the fish canneries, slicing open the pale bellies of tuna, pulling the guts out until the front of her apron was bloody. She had two children, then he left her.

He got married again. Tried to buy a house. "Here's my discharge papers, see?" he said, unfolding the yellow-eyed jaguar animal. "I was Honorable. I can use the GI Bill to get me a house."

The man who sold houses laughed. "You're an Indian!" The yellow-eyed animal crumbled into dust. The paper fell from Dad's fingers.

So my mother tried. "I'm not an Indian. And I've got a job." She looked at the house with its white trim and oleander bushes with yellow eyes and the cracked sidewalk that swam up the street like a gutted tuna and the street that opened into the ocean where war was over for a little while.

The man who sold houses laughed. "You're a woman!" He got into his car and drove away, leaving my parents standing somewhere on a lot of nothing.

Then they saw a woman wearing a black sheath dress, her body like a slim knife, and black high-heeled shoes with small buttons shaped like white horses. Her skin was the color of Los Angeles and she smelled like citrus before the trees were cut down to make room for the tract houses. She stopped in front of them. Her eyes were the sad eyes of a jaguar priest reduced to licking the spilled blood of tequila off the velvet floors of the El Toro bar in Tijuana.

"Someday, your daughter's going to write about this," La Morena promised. "Doesn't matter if she gets it the way it really happened. Nothing happens the way we remember it."

"Yeah?" challenged my mother. "What happened is that we didn't get the house."

La Morena swatted the bees that flew from her fingertips. Her fingers were branches and her heart hummed. She pointed to the houses that were made like orange crates, square slats, where the roots of trees once knew yellow animals and the dark oily shapes that moved silently under the earth. She pointed to the houses that were hammered together overnight, ready for sofas and cribs the next day. Houses that squatted in rows, so unlike the white blossoms of almonds and lemons. There were houses that were boxes of tiny embroidered people and houses that bled. There were houses of illegals who counted their money out of tomato-sauce cans. And there were houses of stars who wrote their names in wet cement and wore the furs of dead animals.

La Morena then pointed to my mother. "Your womb is a house. And your daughter is ready to become alive." Then she sauntered away, hips slipping like waves or earthquakes, her dark skin glowing.

That's why, when the dreams of the ocean come to me, I know it's better to be a woman with my own house inside of me, my heart like a two-roomed house, and my own womb that is filled with the scent of salt and life.

Note: My father was really in the army, but I liked the idea of a desert Indian on board a ship. The incident with the realtor did happen.

Anonymous Is Coyote Girl

From a newspaper photo and article about my godfather, James Moreno, East Los
Angeles, 1950.

(Three police officers took a brutal beating in a wild free-for-all with a
    family, including three young girls.
From left, James, 19, and Alex, 22, in jail after the fracas
on the porch of their home at 3307 Hunter.)

Jimmy is staring off the page, hands in pockets.
A four-button dark shirt. No bruises,
but he looks dazed.
Alex wears a leather coat and a polka-dot shirt,
which is in itself a crime.
Nowhere is there a photo of a young girl
with a face carved like a racetrack saint,
eyes with all bets called off,
grinning like a coyote.

(Officer Parks had his glasses broken
with his own sap
and was thrown through a window.)

Jimmy and Alex are my dad's cousins,
lived on Boyle Heights and tortillas.
Mama says the cops always harassed them, those *niños*
from East L.A., driving their low-riders,
chrome shinier than a cop's badge.
And why wasn't Coyote Girl mentioned, that round-armed
girl with a punch like a bag of bees,
a girl with old eyes, her lips cracking open
as she saw the cop sailing through glass, boiling out
of Boyle Heights, skidding on the sidewalk, flat as a tortilla?

(The officers received severe cuts and bruises,
were treated at a hospital and released in time to jail the youths,
who were charged with assault with a deadly weapon.)

Two years later, I was born and Jimmy entered the church,
hands in his pockets, shoulders hunched, watching the christening.
Four drops of water, like popped-off wafer-thin buttons,
fell on my head.

      No.

He never showed up that day
or any other. My spiritual guardian must've been there
in spirit only.
He didn't know *nada* about God and no one knows
where he is today, but I think you could find him at the end
of a knife. Or in the slash of the *z*
in ¡La Raza! the dark blood
reds of graffiti. Or tomatoes
grown in old coffee cans
by a white-haired man
sitting in the sun in a dark shirt,
next to an old woman growing younger every day
as I tell her story, my story,
our story
with all the grace and power
of a deadly weapon.

The Sharp Smell of Burnt Sugar

LONG BEACH, CALIFORNIA, 1950

When Jimmy and Alex Moreno threw the cop out
the window, Coyote Woman was just a girl,
skin the color of damp sand. *La Morena*:
the Dark One. How they got their name
is forgotten like a key under a stranger's doormat.
It was their only way into themselves,
their dark language
a tunnel under the white city of angels.

¡Híjole! Dark One, remember Silvia's son?
The one who got hooked on morphine
during the war 'cuz he got wounded,
was it in Korea or the back?
You know he disappeared one day.
They found him in the city garbage dump,
another dead mex, with a knife
in his back and the gang boys had smiles
innocent as razors. You think
all Chicanos are wetbacks
and it's true: there's blood behind them.

All the way back to Cortés.

And what about our father's sisters?
Like little Kuti. Or Pilar
who made pies at the factory,
the sharp smell of burnt sugar
caught in her hair like a halo.
They didn't want to be indias,
no Yaqui blood, 'cuz it's better
to be *Spanish* and living
on Signal Hill eating strawberry
jam in rolled-up tortillas, watching the cars

go over the edge, the oil pumping up
outta the ground like bony birds pulling up slick
worms, the oil rigs standing in the Pacific
like bombed-out shrines. ¡Mira! We're sleeping
over the mass graves of dead Chumash
and los vatos from East L.A.
Remember the small woman's bones
found at La Brea. That dark smell
of tar and fear.

Ahora, I understand mis tías. They were before
La Raza and las chicanas feministas.
Once and again, it was better not to be Yaqui.
Better not be sold, killed, enslaved,
spit on, to smell blood burning
bitterly in your children's dreams.
You know, it's better to be alive, Dark One,
you with the rigor mortis smile
inherited from a long family line
of short lives

all the way back to Cortés.

Lost River

OREGON, 1852–1952

1

One hundred years after Captain Jack was gunned down,
unarmed, by Indian hunter Ben Wright,
my mother carries me in her arms
north through Modoc country.
Dad drives the pickup,
his dark forearm resting on the open window,
lava beds on the right,
historical markers on the left,
on a highway paved with bones,
tires singing,
over Indian America.

2

"Ben Wright told them he would like to hunt Indians . . .
so [he] got some men that liked to hunt Indians
to go with him. When they all got together
they numbered over one hundred men. . . .
They all left Yreka . . . to hunt down the Modoc Indians. . . .
Wright traveled all through the Klamath Indian country,
killing
Klamath Indians wherever he could
find them. He went through Goose Lake country,
killed
Paiute Indians wherever
he got the chance. . . .

On the south bank of Lost River . . .
Ben Wright looks along his gun barrel;
he turns slowly around to his men
and says: "Boys, don't spare the squaws.
Get them all!"

The whites shot them
down so fast on the south bank,
they jumped in the river. . . .
When they got about halfway across
the whites on the north bank opened fire
on them. Only five escaped. . . .
The citizens [of Yreka] gave Wright a big dance.
He was . . . the mighty Indian Hunter,
Savage Civilizer, Peace Maker, etc."[1]

3

etc.
etc.
etc.
food for coyotes, etc.
on the banks of Lost River,
on the banks of all the rivers in America
in the America of the Lost.
"Now what shall I do?
Shall I run every time I see white people?"
Captain Jack's father asks. Every Indian asks
this, even those of us who are half-white.
That's why we're always running
away from ourselves
and falling into rivers
some of us escaping,
into the sights of a gun.

4

My mother's white. Her milk is sweet.
Her freckled skin looks like flour tortillas.
Our truck lulls me to sleep, subdues me
as we drive through Klamath country,
past every historical marker Dad ignores
determinedly. My mother carries me
over the unmarked killing grounds:
the highways of America.
We never stop. Dad drives.
He drives. We never stop.

Mom speed-reads a historical map:
If you are Indian,
you are not
here X.

My Little Sister's Heart in My Hands

Part One: Rogue River, Oregon, 1856

"I promised to give you some of our experience in hunting Indians —
a kind of game not often treated of in your journal —
and as the sport has become rather universal
on this coast, every bit of experience will be of service
to the amateur or professional hunter. . . .
A large herd crossed the mountains last winter. . . .
We have caught a great many females or squaws and young,
but the bucks have generally made their escape. . . .
You must [as a hunter] vow vengeance
against every Indian you meet,
but never molest any
except peaceable Indians,
who are unarmed,
and expect no danger;
this is a gallant thing,
when done in the face of public opinion,
law and order.

If an Indian is a prisoner
and charged with some offense,
you go up to him very fiercely
and say, 'You d——d scoundrel,
why did you steal my pantaloons?'
The Indian does not understand
a word of English, but thinks
it's something terrible, looks scared,
and shakes his head. This is proof
positive
of his guilt
and you haul out your revolver
and blow his brains out.

He can't help himself,
for his feet and hands
are tied.
You have done a determined thing,
and henceforth
are a made man."

—*from an editorial in* Porter's Prairie, *May 28, 1856*

Part Two: Rogue River, 1956

We live not far from the Rogue River
where Indian babies were thrown into bonfires.
I'm too young to know this.
Every night, though, I hear the black snakes in the grass
sliding through the meadows toward the river,
their long black bodies gliding, glistening like tears.
Under the pear-shaped stars, in the orchards of womblike fruit,
I hear cries, weeping. I hear Sally Bell's voice:
Soon . . . some white men came.
They killed my grandfather
and my mother
and my father.
I saw them do it.
Then they killed my baby sister
and cut her heart out
and threw it in the brush
where I ran and hid.
My little sister was a baby,
just crawling around.
I didn't know what to do.
I was so scared that I guess
I just hid there
a long time
with my little sister's heart
in my hands . . .

Part Three: Rogue River in Review, 1996

I have a baby sister.
I have a daughter.
I have a mother.
I have a grandmother.
I have felt their hearts beating
under my cupped hands, against my cheek
as I loved them, as I slept.

A long time have we hid
with our hearts in our hands
with the soft red rivers
flowing
from one to the other.
You can't say you didn't know.
Not now. Not now.
And though some have died
not hurting anyone,
they are *this* voice, *this* poem
untied, and henceforth
determined
that the truth
will blow your brains out.

Note: We lived outside Grant's Pass, Oregon, for a few years, my parents logging their land for a living. Sally Bell was a Sinkyone Indian woman, and her report was recorded in 1935.

The Other Story

After she left with the girls,
wearing a dress stained with berries,
he quit working. Quit
pulling down trees. Quit
dragging the logs to the mill.
Bears aren't that ambitious.

He had a honey on the side,
though, a sweet thing.
Blonde, young, thinking he was mythic
and noble. She hadn't gotten fed up
with all his stories yet.

They got married. It's the way it's done.
Girl marries an animal.
The old stories say it happens.
But one day, as she sat,
watching their children
and mending a tear in his coat,
she saw hairs red as sin.
So that night she hid under the stars
and saw him turn himself inside out.
He wasn't a bear!
He was a coyote.
He yowled, walked stiff-legged
under the moon. Got more women
pregnant. Here the story should end
with the moral: Don't marry animals.
Here's a better one: Know the true nature
of the animal you marry.

Note: This poem is about when my mother took my sister, Barbara, and me and secretly left our
home in Oregon. She was afraid of my father. After we left, we drove back to southern California.

Chief Red Feather

[Chief Red Feather] is a Navajo-Sioux Indian who has for many
years greeted the guests at Knott's Berry Farm. His striking
costume is more Sioux than Navajo. To meet this friendly man will
be to better know and appreciate our American Indians.
—*from a postcard with his photo on it, around 1959–1960*

1

He's an attraction, like the "old" ghost town
with its swinging saloon doors,
the house no one can walk straight in
because nothing is level, true,
our eye deceived by a false perspective.
Here in the middle of Orange County,
where houses replace fruit trees in rows
and the air is no longer perfumed with white blossoms,
Chief Red Feather waves *hello*.

Picture him: full Plains headdress, feathers tipped with red,
bone choker necklace, shirt red, pants black,
leather belt with silver conchos, blue breechcloth,
beaded bag, moccasins. A colorful figure.
He's smiling, standing next to a cloud
of pampas grass and a stretched hide
that looks vaguely doglike,
real enough to be plastic.

His real name was James Brady, born
in New Mexico, retired from Knott's Berry Farm in 1983,
died May 28, 1987.
That's all we know of him.
What else was lost
between the years
of posing for photos, enduring

boys yelling "How!"
people asking, "Is he real?"

2

Mom pushes us forward, her two girls,
tells him we're Indian. I'm too shy
to say a word, though he reminds me distantly
of my father, both uneasy in their roles
as Indian men in a white invention.
The chief gives me a postcard of himself,
hand raised in sign language: *hello*.
Years later, I find the card hidden in memories.
On the back, I'd written nothing about him, but:
I pat horses.

Yes, I hungered for horses:
painted ponies with backs curved like bows,
wrapped them around me like blankets, rode
them until they were ruined, frothing
like the yellowed stars.
I rode the backbone of love
so long my thighs were bloody
and if the horses became boys,
I never knew the difference,
my heart false, cantering off center.

3

Once my father visited us,
wearing a silver buckle, rings
bright as horses' eyes,
black flat-brimmed Indian hat.
I ducked my head, not used to his darkness,
only my mother's hair the color of dandelions.

He gave me a half dollar, silver and heavy
in my palm. When he left, Mother stormed:
"No child support, just a lousy half dollar!"

She found out he owned an Arabian horse
north of Tucson and imagined the cost of hay
versus the clothes, shoes her girls needed.
I dreamed only of riding the horse to the mountains
above the desert, my bare feet smooth
against the wide curve of ribs, wind.
I'm the dreamer; I pat horses where none exist.
I invented my life, one man after another.
I forgot my father among the amusement
rides. Chief Red Feather was the only man
who never said *good-bye*.

4

I moved far away, into other houses,
where we hung newspapers for curtains, slept
in borrowed beds. My father had other kids,
mother remarried, sister drank whiskey, gulped pills
until her heart stopped, started again just north
of the state line. I learned to walk straight
past the ghost towns of my childhood,
into the stories that make art level and life true.

Now it's time to see beyond the image
we make of ourselves
and who others believe is real.
So I put Chief Red Feather into this poem
that pounds like a drum and let him beat his way out,
out, until he's neither my father nor memory confused
in a dizzy rain of silver conchos, coins;
no one's Indian, but Jim Brady: man.
Hello.

Bamboo Angels

Smoking candy cigarettes,
I squatted down in the green
light, the bamboo swaying
like long-legged girls.
The desert wind hissed,
hot, the color of saffron.
Los niños couldn't find me.
I heard their prowling,
the wolf whistles,
pebbles rattling down
the cement embankment.

They'd told me a story
about an angel strutting down the street
and disappearing into the bamboo forest.
She wore lipstick the color of cooked lobster,
and wings covered by graffiti.
Every night, she knelt at the river
and washed under her skirt.

I wanted to see an angel.
They laughed, then picked straws
to see who would take me.
When one grabbed me, I ran,
hoping for saints and heavenly hosts.

At the edge of bamboo,
black and white cows mooed,
milk bags swollen,
ears turning like radar.

I ran until my socks fell down,
wadded up in my tennis shoes.
Chewing on the tip of my candy cig,

I waited for the angel
imagining her bright face
like a mirror of my mother's
when she held my face in her two hands.

The grass whispered. Two boys stalked
my trail, big kids with fists like dumbbells.
Panting, one said, *I'll go first.*
You hold her legs.

Were they going to catch her?
I didn't think angels had legs;
they just floated down
from the San Gabriel Mountains,
fanning the smog with their wings,
dodging Klieg lights
in Hollywood on opening nights.

The other kid grinned:
she's a virgin.

I dropped my cig.
Was La Virgen here, too,
smiling, with the red-mouthed angel?
Grass flickered like snake tongues
in my hair. The wind picked up
the sour mash from the pig-feed factory,
bread baking at the Dutchman's.
Los niños moved away, calling
girlie, girlie.

Everything was vertical,
the sparrows rising up the pale
paths, the sun in giant columns,
bamboo stems rustling
like a woman's thighs.
I sat, hearing los niños returning,
closing my eyes so I could see
the angel better. Then a silence,

like a flame snuffed out,
the birds still as stones in the sky,
cows quiet as milk,
the wind dropping into the earth.

A hand reached for me,
then jerked back as angels descended,
shaking the earth, the ground rippling
like the blue robes of the Virgin,
bamboo breaking over the backs
of los niños who ran, skittering,
across the river debris.

I placed my palms on the earth,
in a rain of green leaves,
shuddering as the ground swayed,
smelling the sweat of angels,
the dust from their wings
shining inside me,
and then they were gone.

La Morena and Her Beehive Hairdo

1965–1970

The Dark One sported a beehive hairdo
where she once hid her brother Alfonso.
His girlfriend had a husband who carried a switchblade
pretty as a butterfly in his back pocket.
Alfonso camped out in La Morena's dusky hair
until the coast was clear, at least as far as San Pedro.
Then he vamoosed to Tucson
where he married a young hairdresser
from the Yaqui barrio.

Without any family responsibilities, La Morena felt light-headed.
She changed her name again. *Old Lady*. It was the sixties, man,
and she was everyone's old lady. She really dug those long-haired vets
from Nam. She wore granny boots and long paisley dresses
and carried a small baggie of white horse
in her leather fringed purse. Everyone called her
Indian Princess and said Cher looked just like her.
She slept around, sniffing like a coyote
at every dude's balls, snorting coke up a straw
until she saw red stars galloping around her heart
and herds of tiny white horses dying in nights of Black Velvet.

I won't ask her if she remembers. It was real
but it wasn't true. She was living in someone else's mandala
because it was on the top-ten chart. Somewhere
along the way she lost herself. It's the Yaqui Way
of Knowledge by Carlos Coyote-Peyote.
When we found Jesus, we held out our palms
for coins, Bibles, good-looking Indian boys.
She was my sister. Kneel down, little sister, she said.
And we did, down in front of altars of bees
and tubes of pale lipstick, crosses made of lovers' bodies,

broken shoes, floods of moons, Janis Joplin, rowdy measures
of life. Those summers, slab dancing and picking up guys,
were the best times, she says, the *best*. When she was young
and I was just beginning my own story, my own howling
at the American moon.

La Virgen de Trent Avenue

SPOKANE, WASHINGTON, 1969

Sí, hippie Morena got religion one day
in the back of a VW van with Carlito,
the local Jesus Freaks recruiter,
as they parked out front of the I AM Coffee Shop
where a long-haired dude named Buzz
handed out caffeine and sermons.
We'd met Carlito in front of the Crescent
Department Store where he panhandled
change for Jesus.
Morena put on some fresh lipstick
and we got in the portable prayer room
where we knelt, swaying as the VW
bounced down Main.

Morena told me to get out.
"I got more sin, Carlito," she promised,
"and I need a laying on of hands."
I sighed and left. But Carlito summoned
another sister so he wouldn't be alone
with Temptation.

All week, Morena gave me Dark Looks.

Later, Carlito handed me a Bible and I waited
for him to part the Red Sea.
I prayed for the miracle of Love,
loaves of desire that would rise between us,
multiplying enough to feed our hungry mouths.
Morena glared at my flirting, chewed on her hair,
then her fingernails until she bit the moons off.

¡Ay! Carlito never looked at us again.
He was good at the come-on,
but once we were sisters, nada.

Even so, Morena prayed a lot, kneeling
in front of him. And I knew what
she prayed for as she stared at the crossed
seams of his trousers.

She had it bad, sisters.

Then one day, she told us
she was a virgin
again.
Wore a red T-shirt
with "I Am Goddess"
on it, and a long blue cape
patterned with stars.
Her black shoes curled up
at the toes like crescent moons.
Around her waist, she wore a black belt,
cinched in tight, so her hips moved liquidly
under her pink skirt.
She renounced the male-dominated patriarchy,
"Snakes! ¡Todos!"
and stepped over the I AM threshold,
wiggling her butt adios.

Why Coyote Girl Quit Being a Jesus Freak

1971

Leilani, who was Hawaiian and should've known better,
walked with me down the alley behind Martin's Pawn Shop
on Main Avenue. I nodded to an Indian guy holding up
the building that used to be a Chinese laundry/opium den/
speakeasy/gambling hall but now is Kerri's Kut 'n Klip.
"Hey, sister," he said, afraid to move, his shoulder shoving hard,
holding up the world, brick by brick. I knew another Coyote
had been here. It's an old trick. I could just hear
the Indian guy telling me, "Well, here I was, chasing tail,
around the corner, down the alley, when I saw her backed up
against the wall and puffing hard.
"Hurry," she said, "this building's falling,
and I need a big strong man. Push hard, yeah, that's it.
I'll go get help."
So that's the last he saw of her, but he recognized me,
some part of me, that knew the fool.
"Hey, sister," he said.

"Don't," said Leilani. "Don't speak to strange men."
She tucked a strand of hair more firmly
under her scarf.

He's not strange, I said. Just gullible.

"I mean, don't talk to strangers, and while I'm telling you this,
the Brothers have asked me to speak to you."

About what?

"Your hair is beautiful,"
she said,
"and distracts them
with impure thoughts."

My hair has impure thoughts?

"No, the Brothers have impure thoughts."

About my hair?

"About you, who are attached to your hair,
your beautiful hair, which makes them want
to touch silk."

I could give them a *choni*.

"What's that?" she asked.

It's a piece of scalp, traditionally Apache, with long hair
attached
and braided with red ribbon.
It's not erotic.

"I . . . I wouldn't think so." Leilani looked at me.
"You don't really have one of those
do you?"

No, but I could get one.
If you think it would help.

She stopped walking and turned to me.
"The Brothers told me you must cover your hair
with a scarf,
something plain, maybe black."

Why don't they cover their eyes?

"Because they will only dream
of what they can't see —
your long beautiful hair,
which molds your body
and illuminates like a dark flame
the denial of their desire."

I can't be responsible for their fantasies.
I won't hide my hair
my long beautiful hair
that is straight

that is kinky
when I braid, unbraid it,
that is so like yours, Leilani,
dark, female, and native,
everything they are afraid of.

The Esperanza Sisters, Continued

La Mariposa

Yo soy Dominga, la mariposa. Sí, I'm the butterfly, the woman with the American lover. He was a fine man to look at: hair the color of ripe corn, blue eyes, strong thighs. He had ghost skin, so pale that he reflected a manly moon-glow in the night. The first time I saw him, my heart fluttered. He was leaping in the desert night like a goat on jimson weed. I thought he was demented. In his hand he waved a long net.

I hid behind the cactus. Was he trying to catch stars? Was he a devil? I crossed myself and tried to crawl away, quietly. He was muy guapo, very handsome, but completely loco. I wanted to find the priest. But El Loco heard me and stared straight at me.

"Don't be afraid," he said to me in Spanish. "I'm looking for moths."

His saying *that* didn't prove his sanity . . . what kind of man catches moths? I ran away.

But the next day I saw him talking with Father Borracho, who was scratching his ass and yawning. It was noon and Father slept late. I crept closer and listened. The man was a scientist, he studied butterflies, and wrote about them in books.

I still thought he was a little crazy, but he saw me and smiled. I went to work for him, catching butterflies for centavos. I was young then and impressionable. A pretty face means nothing to me now. When we went to Durango, I rode behind him, rubbing myself against him and moaning. He knew how to spread my legs like delicate wings while I fluttered in his hands.

But when we got to Durango, he sold me to a curio shop. *The Human Butterfly*, said the sign, and the owner put me in his front window with my skirts spread wide. I spat at every man: ¡Chinga tu madre! I swore. After two years, I escaped. In the middle of the night, wearing only a white chemise, I ran into the desert.

All around me, moths blossomed from cacti, tiny bits of wings and pale pure flight, toward the moon's light. I jumped and twirled, my arms wide. For once my legs were clean, my breasts falling and rising only with my own rhythm. I floated into the desert, west, toward the sea and north.

I painted the sea on my face with pigments ground from white fluted shells and red desert sand. I walked to Yaqui land, passing Vicam in the middle of the night.

I didn't want to stay, to see my sisters. I was afraid they'd see how I still belonged in Death's curio shop.

The dogs barked at my soft footfall. I walked through the fields of maize. Some fields were deserted, the maize broken by the sharp heart-tracks of deer. The people had fled into the mountains. Vicam was dark behind me, the stars above loud in the desert, as if each star was a mouth wide open. I remembered we thought the dead become stars. But what can the dead tell us? Why do they want to tell us anything? And why should I listen to those who have abandoned me? I will do the leaving from now on. I will start with leaving my past . . .

In Durango, all day the miners smashed the rocks with their hands or picks. They strangled in dust, swam in the deep humidity of the earth. At night, they came out of the ground, pale as corpses, eyes matted with soil, their fingers smelling like minerals. Then they came to me, to the man who sold me. And the miners dug their fingers into me, churning my insides into mud. They broke off parts of me with each hard thrust, their eyes sealed shut with mica tears. What was I, a woman, a mine, the mother lode? Or another way of burying themselves deep before they were dead?

I became inanimate. A rock. Volcanic in conception. Once a fiery little girl who liked to screech when tickled, I became a pitted rock, still-chambered as the moon. You could find me anywhere in the desert, that kind of rock. Female. Indian. Common as dirt. Yet deep inside, I remembered heat, eruption, the building of continents. I remembered Yomumuli, who made everything and gave us choices: to stay or go?

Escape meant flight. From rock to wings. A rock that flies? Ahh, a falling star. Maybe the dead do come back to us. But who are we? Are we still a people when we are beaten as individuals? There is no tribe anymore. The priests have taken away my nakedness by proclaiming it. The hacienda owners have taken away our freedom. The federales have taken our land. Men have taken away my innocence. I am my own land, my own freedom.

I want to walk north, past Guaymas. I want to be a woman who flows like water, smells like rain, speaks the ancient language of life. I will know only the me I become. That is how my tribe will survive. In the individual's reinvention of life. I am a Yaqui woman; I will define myself. I feel life in my womb. It doesn't matter who the father is. It's *my* child fluttering under my heart. In my daughter's hair I'll weave stars and the fur of mountain lions. I will teach her to walk the vow of life.

Great-Granddaughter of a Butterfly

"Lori," says my great-grandmother, "why are you always wearing black? Don't you know that's an old woman's color?" I just laugh. She used to wear pretty clothes. I've seen some old photos, but now she wraps herself up like one of those women in Iran or something. All black from head to toe. Well, her underwear is white.

I like black. It's very dramatic and brings out my coloring. I like my dark eyes and hair. Sometimes I wish my skin was darker, like my sister Ashley's, but other times I like it just the way it is, kinda like honey. I'm the lightest-colored one in the family. Mom's the color of caramel candy.

I don't know about Dad. I can't remember him very well. He left one night, skipped out into the black-summer, noisy-city, honking-car night. Mom threw his clothes out on the back porch, but he never came back for them. Then she put 'em in the dog's bed. Now when I think of Dad, I think wet, stinky dog hair. Caesar was a nice old dog. When he died we gave him a big ceremony, buried a bone with him that had lots of meat on it. When Dad died, we heard about it from his girlfriend, Sandy, and Mom barked a harsh laugh. I cried because my stomach suddenly fell down to my toes, but, like, no tears would come out. I guess I didn't know him too well. I was just a kid then. He always wore white cowboy hats. Lots of old Mexican guys do that. It must be like some kind of age-costume thing. The old ladies wear black; the men wear white. Maybe life gets down to that by their age. Everything is simple: like it's life or death. That's all there's ever been anyway.

Great-Grandmother tells me a lot about how she walked all over Mexico and that she's the last of the real Yaquis, but she can't talk Indian. So I don't know. Her stories stretch way back, but after her words there's nothing but blackness. History is just a black tunnel to me. She shakes her head and tells me I don't know a thing, not a darn thing. Okay, her stories make everything alive, but when she's dead, then what? She's history, excuse me for being blunt. She just walks down that dark tunnel to nowhere. She always wants me to listen, to understand, to remember. She goes on and on about the old days when she was poor and hungry. "I wore my name on the tip of my tongue," she says, "because it was the only thing I had left of myself."

I feel sad she had a hard time, but it's hard now, too. You gotta dress right, buy the expensive stuff, you know, or get beat up at school. It's a war out there. She just doesn't get it.

My middle name is lame. It's Mariposa and means "Butterfly" in Mexican. There's also a Yaqui word for it but it's too hard to remember.

People think my mother was a hippie to name me that. Mom says I'll be proud of the name someday, when I'm older and can appreciate things. I think I'm old enough now for her to quit talking like that.

They want me to be what they were, but I'm me. I'm an American. I'm fifteen, almost sixteen, and gonna get my driver's license next month. I don't have time to look to the past; I'm my future. Do you see what I'm saying?

Yeah, I'm part Yaqui and it's cool. I like going to powwows and dancing and eating fry bread. But I don't live in the past the way they do. I can be Yaqui and just get on with life. That's what I think anyway.

La Llorona, the Crying Woman

In Mexico and the Southwest, there is an old story about a spirit woman who wanders the desert looking for men. She is very beautiful and sad. When men approach her, trying to help, they are captivated by her beauty and she destroys them. Some say she is seeking revenge for all of her children who were killed by the Spanish conquistadores. Others think that this is a metaphor for the destruction of native cultures and that she is Mexico personified. It's also been suggested that she is Malintzin (or La Malinche), an Aztec sold as a slave to the Mayas and later sold again to Cortés. They say she drowned her son when Cortés wanted to take him back to Spain and leave her in Mexico. In my version, I've put her in the modern, urban world. She has just finished presenting her work before an audience and is answering their questions. Perhaps she is now a poet or an artist.

Thank you. Now maybe you have some questions
you'd like to ask me?
But first let me tell you about my hands
which were once white flowers
and now are rain.
They have the distinctive fragrance
of a woman plucking eucalyptus leaves.

A good question: how do I get my ideas?
I wander the streets looking
for some man dumb enough
to come out in the dark,
when he knows there are ghosts shaped like maggots
and things without any feet
and humans stiff with vomit huddled in doorways,
and I loosen my hair
and weep like an owl.
I wear a gown he can see through
so of course he follows me anywhere,
my beautiful face suspended
above a neck slender as a candle

and he follows, stumbling

hands outstretched like a comic book zombie.
Usually, I take him to the reservoir
although the lake is more traditional,
and I watch the black waters reflecting the moon
until my eyes are swollen with tears.
I slither into the water;
he wades toward me, his mouth gaping like a loony.
The water turns into blood and he's wading up to his hips
in blood, he's drowning in blood.
He thinks this is a Stephen King movie, but it's not.
I'm real. The last thing he sees
is my face looking like a horse's head
stripped of its flesh.

Next question. Am I rich?
Where my mouth was there is fire
and my tongue which was the milky tongue
of many generations
is a bag of dust.
I am not a metaphor for all the Indian women
who have suffered. I'm as real
as your denial, your ignorance.
I am as rich as my daughter whose body was smeared
by the white liquids of men
as my son who suffocated in the red dust of TB
as my baby whose body shook in the black fires
of prophetic dreams
as my unborn whose body was a window for the blue doves
as my twins who slaved in the Durango silver mines
and who whored at the gates for a mouthful of corn
and as rich as the miscarried who died with burning sores
and as fortunate as their children who became instead mimosa
and the strange laughter in the wild wind.

Another good question: Am I famous?
I come from the center of red hands
and my voice is known
in the roots of grass.

question, please.
  What's my next project?
  actually, I've been working on this
for some time: my hands are full of syringes.
There are humans substantial as rags
who suck on my cocaine breasts.
I wipe the pus from the cracks
in their tongues and give them blankets
of paper. I wear my skirt clear up
to my ass so they can see my blood-dark body
and I hook them, flashing
my long red fingernails
that used to be rain
but now are thicker, saltier,
because one's life work must evolve.

I'm confident of the universal impact
of my new work.

Well, I'd like to answer more of your questions
but there's moonlight twitching out of my hair
and some of you are ready for a fix, aren't you,
and some of you have appointments with the dark
hands of strangers so I want you to know
that I've worked through my feelings of revenge.
What I do now, watching you carve up your skin
into totemic white snakes,
is nothing personal:
history was legend is Art.

Thank you for inviting me,
but now, as you know,
your time is up.

Dream-Walkers from the Flower World

(Yaquis believe in a supernatural world of spirit and beauty.)

Ay, the dream-walkers come through the marrow
of blue waters, dancing in the balls of our feet,
necklaces of spidery shells clacking on our chests,
chanting *hiapsi, hiapsi, hiapsi, hiapsi.*

Sometimes we clap our many-colored hands
until the white moons seep out of our locked fingers
and float across the blue doorways with dried red chilies
and the drum skins remember how the wind

smelled like cornflowers. We shake our rattles
of deer hooves, bending lower, cocoons of butterflies
on our ankles, and fly over the hot balconies,
the men bending close to the radios,

the women peeling oranges above the dark exhaust
of the streets, the children jumping into squares, out
of windows young girls cooing at shadows.
We become one with the spirits, swimming with the tides

of whales in green seas, and into the dreams of people.
Oldest dream-walker haunts men with her soft nipples,
shines her big eyes on their sleeping faces, crying,
looking for the one who left her, lying down

beside them until they wake, suffocating,
their hands pushing away a soft darkness.
Black smell, like a dead fish, is another walker.
He/she is a long drape of blood, mourns

like a hard crack of pain with no smooth edges.
He/she chews on dreams, always hungry,
in long cloaks of bones and little child's smile.
So many dream-walkers. There is the virgin

who rises from the mineral waters,
dry every time, her face an icon on the wall,
eyes the intensity of blue bottles
on a windowsill, and everyone begs her

to answer their dreams. She walks through fields
of lettuce and pesticide, blessing the workers
with small medals, kissing their lesions.
Other dream-walkers have feet like clams

and little eyes like soldiers when they're afraid
of knives in the dark and are naked.
Some are like bewitched babies, crawling,
skin glowing rainbows and sparkles.

Some like long journeys deep into people.
Some can't get along without a certain person.
Some wander with circles of paint
around their eyes and long dart pipes,

standing motionless in jungle waters
the color of pepper. Some walk in gray silk
suits and talk suicide. Others see the tattered
faces of people on ledges, bridges,

and soothe them, giving them back their dreams
so that the people see sooty crows flying
over pyramids of lemons and remember
how beautiful life can be.

But some people make a wound of dreams
worldwide
and name it war. They boot clomp
clomp, wearing green

cloth made from plants, then they spray
liquid fire on the dreaming leaves
until all the roots of the world
scream and the scream enters

enters
the black padded cats, the twig-footed canaries,
the heavy-toed elephants, the mudcrust hooves
of cows and the scream darkens the milk

as it's sucked into the mouths of children.
It is the sound all of us become.
We who were the dancers
watching the spirits

are the spirits. Some people burn us
with daggery drugs, breaking
our luminescent bodies into capsules
until their dreams are fragments

of reality. Then we must dream four colors
and dance into the grass
as it makes wavery circles
on the earth. Earth be dreaming all the time,

so that the plants can dream again,
rooting deep into human footprints,
until the shape of man becomes the shape of plant,
and so the animals can dream again,

tusk and horn, antler and whisker,
until the flocks of birds are islands in the sky
and the snakes shine their brilliant
patterned skin in caves and the bats blink,

stretching their leathery wings
across the starry fruiting
singing in high chorus.
Ay, we dream into animals:

the far animals that live reefs away
in other universes:
those that are sealed in vertigo
those that are made of incomplete octagons

dreaming of the missing side,
those that praise creation of its enormous night
those that swim through clouds of mathematical equations
those that growl in their concentrated throats

those that praise creation into the beauty of morning
those with hands like waterfalls
and skin like Peruvian weavings
those with many eyes who see light

as many-seeded, those who live on watery worlds
where rivers run through oceans,
those who tell stories about ancient giants
and little people and they are the same ones.

We dream into earth animals, too,
down into their paws and run without being crippled
and howl without being gunned.
Run in life. Run in death.

It's the same run.
Those red eyes run in dreams
of the hunt when ice dreamed long winters
and we pant with them

our tongues hanging out,
teeth full of strong meat,
bellies full as the moon.
No bright cities then

to dim the lineage
of the starry ones.
Ice still dreaming,
fire still dreaming.

Some people know how to journey
with us. They wear hoods of fur
or feathers or scar their skins
with sacred paths

they paint red ocher
on their cheeks
on the soles of their feet
on their vaginas

where it is a holy memory
of the path out.
They sing and dance
with hands of smoke

until we grasp their wrists
and pull them over
and they hear our drums
coming from their chests.

Some people love earth
and dream flowering altars
and candle-lit stars,
the topography of turtle

backs as they migrate
from the sea to lay eggs.
Some men marry the moon,
swim in cones of flashing fish,

calling women secret names
of great beauty,
humming like bees
in the snow.

There are sisters with white voices
that revere the shed skins of snakes,
white orange blossoms, pale
markings of snails in the dew.

There are sisters with indigo voices
that are the vowels of tattoos
and blue jeans, eggplant and glaciers
at midnight.

We can go anywhere. Into rain
or womb. Into cells of viruses and rivers
flooded with swimming monkeys.
We watch a girl drawing circles

in the red dirt so that ants will get lost
and we see the ants circling the girl
so that she becomes part of their landscape.
We walk in good richness, in

sweet bodies like cherries or caterpillars
or long-eyed girls with perfumed cones
in their hair or boys vaulting over
the golden-skinned cows.

We are here to tell you
that the spirit world is like footsteps
you hear in the next room
and when you get up

you know they are yours.
We are here to tell you
that trees are made of circles
older than you

and that the origin of poetry
is in the larvae of worms
who have spun syllables of silk
from their saliva.

Listen: the stone calendar is without days
and marked by solstices of red feathers
and iridescent dolphins from the Sea
of Cortés. The calendar is not stone

but the music of dark-tailed cats
and the wind winding its way
through an empty snail shell.
The calendar is not music

but an architecture of opposites.
Here we dream away the longest night
and celebrate the gates of wings
birds make in their migrations.

Here we follow the sky paths
into the dreams of those who never wake,
but sleep in green-walled hospitals
and we shake their shoulders

until they come with us, robed
in tangerine-colored clothes
and turquoise shoes with tiny bells.
All earth has corners of sadness,

hands stretched out through barbed wire,
starving-bellied children with ribs
like sabers, men who huddled in tanks
as fire is poured over their homes.

This is what happens when dreams
are broken for nations
and individuals.
All beginnings begin with dreams.

All circles begin with the good night
of stars and the red hands on cave walls.
All loving begins within the dream
of what love could be.

Those who value dreams
place their hands on the face
of the earth and are one body.
All waking is an understanding

of what should be understood.
Dreams are what's behind the mask.
Dreams are the minarets
of the soul.

The Walking Stone

Sally said good-night to her parents. They were listening to the radio. She curled her lip. It was an old radio, turquoise-colored, with a bent antenna. Soon the old man would be snoring.

She closed the door to her room, blocking the noise of the radio's static. She could hear Mama's high voice commenting about something in the news. Mama tried to keep up with the world. Sally didn't want to end up like Mama, selling cheap fake Nike T-shirts to tourists at the street market. Or selling stinking fish, like her old man.

She lifted the edge of her dresser. Under the bottom drawer, she'd taped a little bag of makeup. Black mascara, jade eyeshadow, red lipstick. Carefully, she put on her face. Her real face, she thought, the face of a woman.

She peered into the mirror. She saw a girl with long dark hair smooth as ironed ribbons. Large dark eyes with flecks of green in the irises. Brown skin, a wide mouth. She uncapped the lipstick tube and twisted the lipstick out. It was red, the color of wine and her friend María's dress, the one with two ruffles.

Her real name was Sawali Wiikit, "Little Yellow Bird," but that was so old-fashioned. She had found "Sally" in an American fashion magazine. It sounded modern. *Sa-li.*

The lipstick glided on smoothly. Sally had found it in a lady tourist's purse when the woman was swimming in the water. Sally found lots of things that way.

Now her lips were two ruffles, red and sexy. The American fashion magazine said that it was important to be sexy. There were six articles about it. María's cousin, Estefana, had translated the words, giggling.

Next, Sally layered her lashes with black mascara. She let them dry, not blinking, staring directly into the mirror. Behind her the wall shone like an altar cloth. A crucifix was centered in the middle, the twisted figure of Jesus crying out mutely. He didn't reproach her. He was only a little wooden man.

She applied another layer of mascara. Her eyelashes felt heavy, sensuous. The jade-green eyeshadow was powder. She flicked her tongue on the tip of the brush, wetting it, then swirled the brush in the powder. Beads of jade. Jeweled lids the color of parrots' throats. Or the foamy sea.

She rubbed a tiny bit of lipstick onto each cheek. *Rouge*, her Mama would call it, but the fashion magazines were more modern. They called it "blush." If her father saw it, he would grind it into the earth with the heel of his boot.

Sally looked at herself again in the mirror, then turned toward the window. A dark square, twin to the mirror in shape but without the mirror's vision of the future. Sally was a woman in the mirror. From the window, the sky darkened the garden where Sally had played in the dirt when she was a child. That was the past. Sally wanted to live like the models on the slick pages of the fashion magazines. From the window, bats swooped like soundless accordions. The window was the way to *now*.

She climbed out, dropped to the patio with a soft thud. She rolled up her saffron-yellow skirt, let her teeth shine in the moonlight. Her breasts trembled, each nipple hardening into a tiny plum. Who would touch them tonight, she wondered, lifting their heavy fruitfulness to his mouth?

Wild canaries rustled in the palm trees. Beetles scrabbled across the tin roof of her house. Night breathed in sexual undertones. Layers of darkness, warmth, small tongues tasting the air. Tonight someone would give her perfume, maybe gardenias. And there would be wine, *pitahaya* wine, or some of that good stuff from los Estados Unidos. Jugs of Gallo. María had connections.

That's what it was all about. Even Mama and the old man would agree. It was who you knew in this world. Not who you were or what you knew.

Although . . . she *was* learning a lot in the dark and there were many hands who taught her. Some of them were sons of wealthy men. Or wealthy men themselves. María knew everyone. María in her small house by the golf course, where she made wine and invited close friends to party. María knew everyone worth knowing, the American tourists looking for a good time with a sweet local girl, or the old men who lived in the hills surrounded by high walls and servants who removed their dusty shoes.

Sally wanted to be rich enough one day to be able to throw away a shoe that got dirty.

The next morning, Sally crawled back over her windowsill. She was tired but smiling. Her mouth was bruised from a clumsy kisser. She had kept him from doing the final thing, but with great difficulty. She herself was weakening every night, wanting it all. There had been music, on a fine stereo system with two speakers big as mules, and lots of midnight wine, smudges of her lipstick on the rims of glasses, or on a man's cheek. Someone had given her a tiny vial of honeysuckle cologne, which she had dabbed between the humid valleys of her breasts. All night the men hovered like bees.

Now she wanted to sleep, to dream of the next night, and how maybe a man from Hollywood would come to María's party. "You look like a movie star," he'd say, "let's go to my studio and make you famous." Sally was sure it would happen soon.

"Sawali! What are you doing, you bad girl?"

Her mother stood by the bed. Sally finished climbing over the window and sank onto her bed.

"Where have you been? And look, what's on your face?" Her mother grabbed her by the shoulders. She spat on the hem of her blouse and began to scrub Sally's cheeks.

"Mama, stop that!"

"You're stinking! ¡Borracha! You've been drinking wine!"

"So? I'm not a baby anymore."

Her mother cried, square shoulders shaking. She suddenly straightened up and slapped Sally.

"You will not be a bad girl! No, no! I won't allow it. Wait until I tell your poor father. Don't we work hard all day for you? How can—"

But Sally was asleep, her mouth slack, fumes of wine floating up. Sally's mother backed away, her heart a heavy stone. How she remembered carrying this little one in her arms, the bright eyes staring straight into her soul. Such a beautiful child, her mother's last child, full of laughter. And always so happy, singing . . . just like a canary.

Now, *ahora* . . . Sally's mother smoothed the hair away from her daughter's face. The mascara smeared, the lips swollen, green slashes on the eyelids. She went to get a wet cloth and carefully cleaned her daughter. She found marks on the neck, some man's mouth. It was a shame, shameful.

Some kind of cheap perfume. Torn underwear. Skirt with wine stains. A stink of corruption.

That night, Sally went out again. Another party. An invitation to go on a yacht. Night like silk wings. She sauntered past the church with its white domes and dusty plaza, down the paved walkway to the harbor. A sunburnt man waited for her in a dinghy, *el bote*, smoking American cigarettes, knocking the ashes into the sea. He grunted hello, cigarette clamped between his teeth, and twisted around to cast off. She tottered on her high heels as the boat rocked. Her rear slapped down abruptly on the wooden seat from the thrust of the outboard motor. The man eyed her, squinting through the smoke, and the dark waters sprayed across her knees. He steered the boat toward a yacht strung with tiny white lights.

From aboard the yacht, Sally could see the fishing boats heading back to shore. Guaymas had lots of shrimpers. Her father would be luminous with silver fish scales, blood stiffening the laces of his boots, his black eyes weary. A dog's life, she said to herself, then forgot about the old man as she lifted a glass of wine to her lips. Someone called her name, laughing, while the waves slapped against the boat, rocking it gently. She turned back to the party with a loud squeal as the wine sloshed out of the glass.

"More wine!" she yelled. She staggered to someone's lap and nuzzled his neck. There were many stars out tonight, all of them falling magically into her wine glass. She tilted it up, her throat burning from the heat.

When she stumbled home in the early morning, her father was waiting for her. His rage shook the insects off the roof.

"Get out of this house! If you can't respect us, then leave."

"With pleasure! I'm leaving and never coming back!"

Her mother wailed, hands outstretched. Stone-eyed her father faced her, pointing to the street. Sally clenched her fists and ran.

"Whore!" shouted a neighbor boy. He threw a pebble at her. "¡Puta!"

The whole neighborhood stood outside, silent. Even the birds were still.

Sally ran down the street. Turning the corner, she ran, tears of rage half blinding her. What did they know about being young and full of life! Well, she didn't need them. She had lots of friends. She slowed down, wiping her nose with her hands.

There was her old teacher, Señor Borrring, coming down the street with his cardboard briefcase.

"Sawali! What's wrong?" he asked, shocked at her appearance.

"I'm leaving home, that's what, I'm tired of being treated like a child!" she screamed.

"Oh, por favor, it can't be so bad." He held out his hands, the briefcase dangling sadly.

"I won't go back."

"Parents and children often see things differently. Say you're sorry, that's a good girl, and everything will be all right. God will forgive you anything, why not your parents, child?" He looked at her kindly.

"I don't want to go back and I don't want their forgiveness and I don't want God's forgiveness and I don't want you telling me what to do either! Go to hell!"

"Por favor, I beg you to ask God for guidance!" Her former teacher was so distressed that small flecks of spit fell on his beard.

"I'd rather be a rock than ask God for help, you stupid old man!"

As soon as she spoke, she felt the edges of her world rounding. Her body lost its softness, breasts, belly, thighs thickening the minerals within her. Her heart contracted into a geode. The blood slowed in ruby veins, teeth turned to crystals, skin hardened into brown stone. Her flashing eyes winked into mica. Sawali Wiikit, Little Yellow Bird, was a rock.

You might find the rock rolling along the streets of Guaymas, looking for good times. Pick it up and put it in a mesquite tree, out of harm's way. But don't expect it to be there again when night falls. Some have even put it in front of *la iglesia*, the church, but the walking stone never stays near God and his old man's ways. The walking stone likes bright lights and the rich laughter of women drinking wine, the deep voices of men promising gardenias and diamonds at midnight, when darkness parts her wide legs, and no one has to go home at dawn.

Note: This is a modern version of an old story.

A Good Journey Home to Vicam

SONORA, MEXICO, 1998

The coach pulled up to Vicam, the brakes sighing, then the doors swinging open. The bus driver stood up, stretched, then stepped out. I watched him enter *la tienda*, the store, where red paper valentines were pasted to the protective grillwork across the wide windows. A young girl carrying a tray of white Styrofoam cups filled with fresh shrimp and wedges of lemon got onto the bus. She had tints of red in her short hair and dark eyes that looked beyond us, the passengers sitting quietly with our purses and packages.

"Aquí," said a thin man, and hitched himself forward, reaching into his back pocket for his wallet. She handed him a cup of pink shrimp, and a white napkin.

I looked out the window again. An old woman sat on the store curb, a cardboard box tied with string on her lap. She wore a tiered blue skirt, edged with lace. She was one of the "old" Yaquis, maybe didn't even speak Spanish, I supposed. Around her shoulders, like the wings of a green parrot, was her *rebozo*, a long shawl. She looked right at me, but I knew it was my imagination because the bus's windows probably reflected the light. Besides, I was wearing sunglasses. So she couldn't see *me*, not my eyes, my mestiza eyes that were corn colors and part parrot feather and partly dark as *un nuez*, a nut. Just in case, though, I closed them. Thought about my trip here, to see the land of the Yaquis, where *mis abuelos*, my grandparents, had come from.

Yesterday, I'd walked along the white sandy beaches, picking up seashells shaped like ice-cream cones and Chinese fans. The turquoise water was warm; pelicans floated companionably, their large feathers drifting to shore. I'd walked to an inlet where the water rushed in and out from the sea, forming a lagoon behind the dunes. A snowy egret poised above the water, still as my breath.

Along the beach, soft red slabs of stone emerged from the crushed shells. This was bedrock, the gentle and elemental basis of land, and it was shaped like a beached whale.

Somewhere, out in the Bay of Sea Serpents, there were supposed to be gray whales and dolphins, but I hadn't seen any, only the boats of the shrimpers.

The desert met the sea, went into the sea. Or the sea became the desert without the water. Any way you looked at it, it was vast. The *monte* was littered with broken shells and pitted volcanic rock. Long ago, an earthquake had split Baja California away from the mainland, allowing the sea to rush in. Volcanoes still dotted the sea as islands, but they slept under the white stink of guano. Instead of sea kelp, the desert had many-armed cacti. The monte, the desert, rose up into mountains, some shaped like pyramids. The colors were white, red, and dusty green. The colors of Mexico.

Yesterday I walked two miles through the desert, past the lagoon where oysters were harvested and eaten raw for breakfast by the visiting gringos, heedless of hepatitis, past the abandoned adobe casa where an osprey perched eating its breakfast of fish, past the muddy puddles left over from a big spring storm (blame it on El Niño). I'd seen a rainbow earlier, which is really the bow of the yellow-haired dwarf Suawaka. He lives in the sky and shoots arrows of lightning. I saw Tetakawi, a twin-peaked hill, jutting up toward the horizon. In San Carlos, they told the tourists that Tetakawi meant "goat's tits" and that it had been blasted out more than intended by the film crew for *Catch 22*. But I also heard that Tetakawi actually means "rock mountain," so I don't know.

I was still thinking about it, sitting on the bus to Ciudad Obregón, where I wanted to see the Yaqui Museum. It was a long ride. I had already taken a smaller bus, with La Virgen de Guadalupe on the dashboard, to Guaymas. Then I transferred to a larger bus. This big coach came with its own TV. We had been watching *Air Force One*, with Harrison Ford, who is muy guapo, until we pulled into Vicam. It is one of the eight Yaqui pueblos.

The bus driver got on again, followed by that old woman who'd been thinking about someone strange. Or maybe a stranger. Me, either way. I knew it because she sat down next to me. She smelled like *yerbas buenas*, sweet grasses, and blue sky. There were many empty seats, but she sat down next to me. I wondered why or what I should do if she started speaking to me. Mi español es malo. My Spanish isn't so good. My Yaqui is practically nonexistent.

She shifted in the seat, smoothing her skirt, settling the box on her lap again. Maybe it was her purse. I amused myself by listing its contents: an ancient silver comb from a spirit cave, a tiny mirror that reflected evil, a cross made out of rooster bones, matches that breathed sulfur, little charms made from soft gold (a hand, a penis, a leg), maybe some hiak viva, Yaqui tobacco grown on the Río Yaqui, rolled in a corn husk and tied with a thread in the middle.

I nodded to her and said "Lios em chania," which was most of the Yaqui I knew. It was a form of greeting with god in it.

She smiled and said it back to me. Then we were silent. The bus shifted gears, backing out, a dog barked, someone waved good-bye to the bus. The TV screen was dark. I turned toward the window, watching the landscape fly by. A movie came on the TV, some Hollywood movie with cops saying "Shit!" a lot and a chicana officer kicking ass. The subtitles were in Spanish and I read them, wanting to learn all the universal bad words. Somehow "¡Mierda!" didn't have the same explosive expression as "Shit!" I took off my sunglasses, opened my backpack, and searched for some gum, something sweet for my mouth.

Wordlessly, I offered a stick of rainbow-colored gum to the woman. She smiled. "Gracias," she said.

"You're welcome," I said automatically, then added "I mean . . . uh, de nada."

"Hablo inglés," she said, nodding and unwrapping the gum. The paper rustled softly against her fingers. She had long hair, tied back in a knot of streaked gray and black. She folded the gum into hills and valleys, then popped it into her mouth. She nodded again.

"Muy bueno, good, thank you very much," she said.

I smiled. A smile is a universal blessing.

From the TV, I heard a car squealing and gunshots. In the aisle across from me, two teenage Yaqui girls sipped red cans of Coke, watching the action. I had the feeling they were off to the big city of Obregón for a little action themselves. They wore lots of eye makeup and layers of lipstick. But they were still very pretty.

The woman next to me breathed out the fruity gum flavors: mango, strawberry, lime, watermelon. I chewed quietly, feeling the juices tart against my tongue.

"Sí," she said, "I espeak good English. I lived in El Norte for many years. Now I come home to live the last time."

She patted the box. It sounded like a drum. Boom, boom. A box that seemed to lose its squareness with the sound, becoming rounder.

I told her that I had come to see the land of my grandparents. I wanted to feel the connection between the past and the present.

She raised her eyebrows, turning in the seat in order to see me more clearly. "Your grandparents de aquí?"

"Sí," I said, "they were Yaqui."

She pointed to herself. "Yo, Hiaqui." She said it back in her throat, as if the tribal name was so ancient it came with its own volcanic explosion. "I live many years in L.A. I worked cleaning houses. Entonces, I married a good man. We had children, dos, but they died. M'ijo was killed in Vietnam. He was a medico. M'ija was in a car accident last year. Mi esposo es muerte, también. There is nada for me there ahora, so I come home. Now I live aquí."

I didn't know what to say. It sounded like a sad life.

"I'm sorry about your children," I said.

"Their candles went out, pfff!" She tapped the box again. A hissing sound, the smell of burnt candle wax. I sniffed again: nada. I chided myself for my overactive imagination.

We sat quietly for a while. I looked at the poor houses that lined the highway. Some were made of sheets of tin and cardboard. The yards were tidy, though. We passed through more desert. I saw a few wild dogs clawing apart garbage tossed from cars. White dogs with ribs the wind could pluck for a mournful howl.

"Where are you staying now?" she asked me.

"In a condo near San Carlos but closer to Guaymas."

"Pues, you must be careful, cuidado. Near Guaymas is a hill with two heads, dos cabezas, called Takalaim. Serpents live there. They make a new head each year. They were bad people once, brothers and sisters married to each other. Ay, no good, so they were worms that made themselves bigger, comprende? And when they have seven heads, they come out of the hills as big winds, like the one we had last night."

The wind had been so ferocious last night that I could feel the surf pounding under my bed.

I nodded.

"Entonces, Suawaka shoots them with his arrows. He kills the wind-serpents and takes the meat up to feed his family. His wife's father is Yuku, full of thunder. His wife's mother is the rain. They eat serpent meat up there in the sky."

"I know about Suawaka," I said.

"Mi primo was fishing near Guaymas a long time past. He saw Suawaka kill a big serpent. Suawaka took mi primo, his name was Rudolfo, up to the sky house. Suawaka was small but strong, you know? He carried Rudolfo and the serpent up to the house. Mi primo said it smelled bad and ¡ay! there were big pieces of meat all over, with scales on them. The Rain Woman said to Rudolfo, *eat!* But he couldn't. It was too bad, he knew the meat was from bad people. There was nada for him to eat, so she said, *You will die here. Go home.* She told her one-eyed husband to give Rudolfo a scale, to show people what it was like. Then, she said, no one will want to fly up here again. So Rudolfo got on top of Suawaka's shoulders and went back to earth again." The old woman looked at me. "And that is why I never go on an airplane. It is too high up and the shiny scales of the sky are not for people. I always go by bus."

I told her, "I had to take three airplanes to get to Sonora. It was a long day and very bumpy."

"Pues," she said, "when you were up there, did you want to eat any of the food?"

"No," I said, remembering how the plane had been tossed around by the storm. I'd felt like throwing up.

She peered at me. "Ahhh, mira, it is true, then!"

I laughed, nodding. She drummed the box again. It sounded like hard pellets of rain, or bullets. There must be more stories in there, I thought. She liked talking. Maybe she lived alone and didn't talk much. Lots of old people are like that.

On TV, the chicana cop was kissing a tough-looking man. "Querido," she whispered to him as she slipped her gun out. His eyes were closed, but he felt her move and threw her down. She shot at him and missed. They were, for some reason, inside a boxcar on a fast-moving train. He shot at her. The bullet went out the door. It whizzed past the cameramen and the yellow-haired dwarf who was an extra in the movie and past the sound technician who was Yuku, providing the thundering train noise. The bullet followed the freeway south to San Diego, then crossed over the border, undocumented, but lethally sure of its right to a better life in Sonora: I was sure I could hear it rattling in the box on an old lady's lap on a bus to Ciudad Obregón.

The woman pointed with her chin to the TV. We watched the chicana cop hanging onto the outside of the speeding train. Her hair streamed behind her. She looked like a flag with legs.

"Mi primo Malon Yeka flew once," she said.

"Where did he go? L.A.?" I asked.

"¡Ay, no!" She chuckled. "He was a smart man, mi primo Malon Yeka. His name means Prairie Dog Nose, I don't know why he was called that. But he was a little loco, maybe a brujo-wannabe!" She laughed again.

"Qué?"

"Pues, he had power dreams, full of flying like an owl in the night with two eyes tunneling into darkness. He flew down those tunnels into the earth, he said, and found the roots of red dreams and old paths north. He found rooms sizzling with snakes and full of sticks with blue flowers."

"Was he un curandero?" I asked. A kind of doctor-shaman.

"No, no, he was muy lazy."

I took out my gum and wadded it up in a piece of Kleenex. It had lost its flavor.

"Mi primo had a family with many children, but he dreamed all day. No work. One day, he let his thoughts fly up. There were many birds flying and he wanted to be like them. What an easy life they had! Flying in the warm air all day, floating. Malon Yeka heard a voice. A buzzard sat next to him. ¡Ay! Was he surprised! The buzzard said, 'Malon Yeka, what do you wish for?'

"Mi primo said, 'Why, to be just like you! A bird who can fly high.'

"The buzzard said, 'Your wish is granted. Here.' And he took off his cape of feathers and gave it to Malon Yeka. Mi primo took off his pants and shirt and shoes and handed them to the buzzard, who said, 'Sí, this suits me!'

"Mi primo put on the feathers. He was muy excited. But the buzzard warned him that life was hard. 'Death is all around us,' he said, 'but it doesn't come often enough to please a buzzard.'

"They said adios. The buzzard put on tight, hard shoes. He hopped around, flapping his elbows. His children laughed at him. His wife told him to get out of the hot sun, he was loco enough as it was. She made him sleep outside because his breath was so bad. In the morning, he couldn't eat the tortillas y frijoles because they weren't dead enough.

"The man who became a buzzard, mi primo loco, was also having problemas. He was mucho hungry. He spent all of his time looking for squashed snakes on the highway to Ciudad Obregón or for dead burros on the monte. He didn't have time to fly high. When he found a dead dog, it was too skinny to eat. The flies attacked mi primo, swarming up from the broken ribs of el perro, the dog, and it smelled awful. He tried to eat the dead dog and its flesh melted in the sun, but he couldn't. He became very hungry.

"Finally, the buzzard and the man who walked with his elbows out like wings met again. 'This isn't working,' they agreed, and so they became themselves again. The buzzard flew away and Malon Yeka returned to his house."

"Did he still dream?" I asked.

"No, he was without dreams and labored in the field until the day he died."

I couldn't tell whether she thought this was good or bad. I liked him dreaming, diving into the subterranean passages where snakes flicked their forked tongues among blue blossoms, and bees hummed like volcanoes.

"Sí, he was mi primo, a smart man, but not wise," she said. "And that is another reason why I never fly."

My mouth twitched into a smile. Every story was a lesson to her.

"I never eat things that had a face," she told me. "When I was a maid in L.A., the woman taught me how to eat without meat. It's better for you. I could never be a buzzard."

I laughed again.

"Y, buzzards are bald up here," she rubbed the top of her head. "No es pretty for a woman!"

She laughed at herself this time. Her skin was gently wrinkled, a soft reddish brown. Her eyes were dark as coffee beans. She was missing a few teeth, and when she talked, I could see the rainbow gum flashing in her mouth like a parrot in a broken cage.

I suddenly realized that I hadn't introduced myself and here we were pulling into Ciudad Obregón.

"Me llamo Anita."

"¡No! *Me* llamo Anita!"

We stared at each other. Which of us had spoken first?

The bus crawled slowly toward the central de autobuses, rocking as it passed over big potholes in the terminal driveway. There were many buses in front of us. It would take a few minutes for our turn.

"So," said Anita, "there is your connection, m'ija!"

And that is why I had flown here, to find the land in the stories my family had told. And haven't I learned that the stories are also in the land, from the two-headed hills where incestuous serpents slept, to las casas in the sky?

The bus driver called out, "Ciudad Obregón!"

The TV movie finished on cue, the chicana cop holding a smoking gun in one hand, tugging on her pantyhose with the other. Dead men lay at her feet. The teen-age Yaqui girls talked muy rápido while they put on more lipstick, their fingers following the flight of their words, reddening the air in front of their mouths.

The old woman took out her gum and stuck it under the seat.

"Por favor," she said. "Do you have children?"

"Sí, dos. Una hija y un hijo."

"Ahh, pues, maybe you can help me. I want to buy a Barbie doll for mi primo's primo's daughter. She wanted a Stewardess Barbie, but I say no. Flying es no good, eh?" She laughed. "I'm old and don't know about Barbie dolls. I want a nice one, comprende? A Good Girl Barbie. No el cheapo."

Did she mean she didn't want a cheap Barbie, one who smoked and stood on street corners, asking all the Kens if they wanted a date? Get a grip, I told myself. Maybe she meant she was willing to pay for a good Barbie, not a Tijuana rip-off. Under all my semi-humorous wonderings, I was aware of my prejudice. I hadn't thought a *real* Yaqui would even think of Barbies. What had I imagined little girls played with? Dolls made of turtle bones and rags?

"How can I help?" I asked.

"Does your hija have a Barbie doll?"

I sighed. It would be embarrassing to admit that she had fourteen Barbies, so I simply nodded.

"Pues, what is the best Barbie? Es muy especial, por una chica, a little girl's birthday. Will you come conmigo to la tienda and help me find one?"

"Claro que sí," I answered without much thought. The Yaqui Museum could wait another hour or so.

The Old Woman With My Name smiled, tapping the box. It was quiet, full of expectations.

"Gracias, I have brought this box to carry una Barbie doll. We will wrap her up in white paper and wish her a good journey home to Vicam."

No Me Recuerdo las Palabras Ahora

It's true. I don't remember
the words now. But Spanish wasn't my mother's tongue;

she spoke Buttemontana, her words as coiled as a copper anaconda:
wrastlin', cunslur, mearer.

My father spoke Spanish in his fingertips, cooking chiles rellenos
and tamales: *¡ven aquí, la comida*!

At Las Flores Elementary, my sixth-grade teacher, Mr. Atwood, taught
    Spanish
fifteen minutes every Friday after he quickly misread the lesson:

tacko, peelota, bate bate las cabezas.
So we beat our heads with balls, bounced tacos off the blackboard,

snickered *¡adios, la cucaracha*!
while he counted on his fingers: *uno, dos, tres* . . .

Now I can be tongue-tied in many languages.
Lios em chania. Tetakawi. Sewa.

Jeg er dumb i dansk, norsk, svensk.
Yo me stúpido en español.

Eller englesk, las palabras
bouncing around inside my brain

like rubber chiles, plastic herrings,
scattered Scrabble tiles. So don't ask me

to tell you who I am based on what tongue I speak.
It's very simple, after all. The tongue is soft tissue

and unlike the heart, it can learn new ways to beat,
bate bate, and savor the spicy words

of many cultures. *Yo soy una chicana,*
una Yaqui, una india, una mestiza,

a woman with a hydra-headed tongue.
Cut one off and I'll grow a new one.

Cut them all off, take away all my words
pero recuerde: Silence is the first indigenous language.

It is the tongue of secrets, thick fruit, red hands,
the dolphin-eye of the human fetus

swimming in salty waters, practicing
its first sound between heartbeat and poem.

Note: This poem is written in Spanish, English, Yaqui, and Danish (which I also speak).

The Humming of Stars and Bees and Waves

Long ago, there was a spirit woman and her name was Yomumuli, Enchanted Bee. She made the earth: the rippling grasses swaying in the wind and the scarlet mountains floating in clouds of tiny blue birds. And the day was divided into astonished animal faces, and the night was a fountainhead of stars and the slumber of river turtles.

Since that time, the papery husks of stars have fallen into the seas and mothers have grown older. Rosa is a woman who talks to herself. Although she doesn't remember the first creation, she does, of course, remember the birth of her only child, a son named Natchez.

She made the people and put them in a village. And in the middle of the village was a Talking Tree that hummed like bees.

When Natchez was little, he talked to his shadow, and Rosa talked with the coyotes and ravens and flowers. But now she is old and can't see very well. Once she caught herself talking to a discarded gum wrapper, thinking it was a flower.

I wonder, she thinks, if my dreams can tell me how to make my eyes better. She knows that her tribe believes in dreams, but since she's half Yaqui, she doesn't always know whether the dreams believe in her. Still, she begs for a dream that would speak healing words. One night she dreams the words "unlined cell differential" and has no idea what they mean. I probably got someone else's dream, she thinks. Another night she dreams about fog, and when she wakes up, her eye is cloudier.

The tree spoke a sacred language. No one could understand it. Not the youngest. Not the oldest. Not the wisest or bravest or strongest. Not even the oldest.

Rosa wakes one morning and remembers a dream that tells her to enter a cave. Grandmother Spider Woman tells her to bring cedar, tobacco, and corn. No walkie-talkie. No flashlight. No strings or bread crumbs to mark the path. Just blind faith.

And so, when the moon is yellow and the mist low under the dark apples . . . when the fields are gold and dry with rows of stars shining on the tassels . . . when the horizon is lilac and the mountains to the west are blue-black, Rosa ties the bag with the offerings around her waist and hikes up the trail to the old caves. The caves are usually there, but legends have it that they sometimes disappear. Rosa is not sure what to expect, so she mutters to herself as she walks.

The back of her neck is hot and sticky, even though the air is cooling and rising from the valley. The trail gets steeper and narrows to one foot in front of the other. She puts one hand on her knee in order to propel herself forward on the steepest part and prays that the rest of her will follow.

"Damn stupid thing to do," she mumbles. She's a little worried about bears, even though one of her husbands had the spirit of a bear. He loved to sleep and eat. That's how she saw people: this one a bull, that one a St. Bernard. But in the past few years, she's been feeling too old for the foolishness of love and friendship. After all, she has herself to talk to and she's a good listener who always agrees with her sentiments. Now, at least the talking will keep away the bears, although she knows you should also wear bells around your neck. However, finding the cedar was hard enough. She ended up using the cedar shavings you use to keep away moths.

Finally, she rounds the curve of the mountain. Her heart is beating fast. The cave opens in front of her like a huge toothless mouth. She can feel the cold, musty air push out toward her. The floor of the cave is rough, littered with angular rocks.

She's a small woman with bony knees and one shoulder slightly higher than the other, but her skin is surprisingly smooth for her age and her hair is still thick. She waits until her heart calms down, then notices it's getting dark outside. She might as well go in.

I hope I know what I'm doing, she says. Walking with her hands spread out in front of her, she hears water rushing to her left. A swift underground stream rushing out into the twilight. Don't let me die in here, she prays.

When Yomumuli returned from her creating, she shook off the images of shimmering feathers and jungle greens and small monkey faces, and loosened her fingers from speckled granite and purple-spiked sea urchins, and brushed off the coral sands from her memory, and listened to her children.

They were worried. They had been given something sacred and had not understood it. Some argued that the holy is never understood.

Rosa listens. The stream has a voice and it chants: *earthbowl* and *duskwomb*. The walls have a voice that rumbles: *terra-cotta hands* and *eyes of clay.*

Rosa feels the presence of tiny spider women, sitting with their spindly legs crossed. Minerals drip, drip, into funnels of teethlike spikes, vaginal and wet. The spider women unlid their thousand eyes and reach out, sticky fingerlings, silken threads slivering the cracks of deeper darkness. The threads anchor Rosa, the out-worlder. The voices are those from the void: *terra marina, terra noche*. Words from the beginning, when all that was, was not spoken. Land. Sea. Night. In Rosa's ears, she hears the bull-roarer and the raw rushing out of a water drum. It is music as old as the heart.

My own body is full of minerals, she thinks, and thousands of her cells echo the stratification of the earth. She isn't lost.

Yomumuli puts her cheek to the Talking Tree and listens to the humming voice.

Rosa is a stone woman. She is a stone fish swimming through a river of turquoise. A half-blind fish, finny and leaping to the rhythm of a shadowless current. She is aware of the tribes of ghostlike fish and frogs that live in the dark waters, sunless, white creatures that dream only of the moon.

When she was a young woman, she liked men. She still likes men, but none of them will look at her. They don't like old women. When she was young, she needed a cane to walk sometimes. Her sight was good, but not always her insight. She often chose the wrong man. Now, she's got a bad eye and it's life that is lame.

There's more than blood in her veins now. There's experience and wisdom and a deep longing for more life. More stories. More kisses.

She remembers her own grandmother, who lived alone for forty-six years after her husband died, celebrating his birthday with flowers in front of a silver-framed photo and yearly visits to the cemetery. Now Natchez has a baby and Rosa sleeps alone, her husband of thirty years dead for some time. She remembers his nightly whispers to her before they fell asleep. One of his favorite sayings was "Life has no guarantees." But, she admits to herself now as she struggles through the cave, she expected life to continue while she was alive!

I've been on the shelf too long, she says, I've gotten dusty.

Yomumuli heard what the tree was saying. She turned to look at her people and spoke, shrug-ging a cloud from her shoulder: I'll tell you what the Tree says but you must promise to believe me!

Rosa trips and falls to her knee. There's blood and a sharp pain. Shit, she moans. She feels old, old as the clay shards in the lap of the earth, old as the curled fetus shapes in red clay graves, skin wrinkled over thin ribs, and all around, faces of grief. Terra Recepta. Corpus terra. The earth is made of beginnings and endings.

I'm not crazy, she repeats to herself. I'm here for a reason. I know what I need, to see, but not how to do it.

Inching forward, her knee throbbing, she feels the walls narrowing. Then the stream widens into a pool; she can hear the stillness in the center and the rushing out near her feet. The spider women throw a ball of moony webs up into the air, and a soft light fills the cave's inner heart.

So, now what do I do? asks Rosa.

Do you believe in us? click the spider women.

Of course! Of course! And so the people listened; the Tree told the animals how to live . . . that the deer should eat grass and the puma eat the deer. Then it spoke about the future when men from a far country would come and everything would change. There would be new laws and new deaths, and a great metal snake with smoke plumes would race across the land. When the people heard this, they became afraid.

Being half-Yaqui isn't easy, Rosa thinks. You have to believe that trees and rocks and birds talk, and you have to have faith in glass-walled elevators and voices transmitted from space. Then there's pantyhose that assumes your shape and dreams that struggle to shape your awareness.

Long ago, Rosa got real tired of shape-changing: being Indian with Indians and white with the whites. As she got older, she became less afraid and howled like a coyote in heat whenever she damn well felt like it.

From the ceiling of the cave, tree roots hang down in a gnarled nest. The cave seems to be breathing feathers, eggs, and clouds.

I believe, whispers Rosa.

Some didn't believe Yomumuli. So she left, with her favorite river rolled up under her arm, walking north, her feet like two dark thunderclouds.

Rosa thinks about her white mothers, their names rolling off her tongue like pearls of barley: Jean, Ann, Yohana, Marija, Barbara, Ana, Margareta, Elizabeth, Susie, Giuliana, Anna, Orsola, Felicita. And her Indian mothers, whose names are rich with corn and chilies: Charlotta, Estefana, Empimenia—and others whose names were lost, unwritten, but remembered in a certain flash of eye.

Rosa feels the Grandmothers' eyes all around her. She sees with their eyes. She sees the pond, its water clear as spiderwebs.

And some of the people went to live in the sea, their whale songs, tubular and roiling, boom-echo and deep in the interior seas of their throats, longing and sounding all in a moaning song, floating up to the spume moon.

Rosa turns to the cave walls. Clay. She pulls a chunk out and rolls it in her hands, forming a ball. Little clay baby. Cave navel, lodestar, and mother lode. She pinches it into a rough bowl. With her thumbs she shapes it, smoothes it.

Quickly, she fills the bowl with pond water. A sip. It tastes like metal and semen and breast milk. It is sour and sweet and musty and white and black and red and yellow.

And some became flying fish, ringing the waves, sparkling, and others became the singers of the sea, with their long hair and rainbow skin. They say that if you're lost at sea, these creatures will help you because they remember the time when we were all one people.

Rosa unties her bag of offerings and puts the tobacco in the bowl. The cedar chips to the right, the corn to the left. Fumbling a bit, she pulls out a book of matches and carefully lights the tobacco. A thin, handlike smoke rises. She has no idea what to do next, or if what she's already done is right.

She thanks her family. She thanks her guardian spirits. She thanks her own strength, which has brought her this far without breaking her neck. She thanks the creator who gives her dreams and daily breath.

The Grandmothers sing: *Ebb and return, web and wheel, smoke and water, the void has wings, we sing and reel. Spinner and spinal songs, spiraling, symphonic, and symbiotic, sightless but full of vision, we Grandmothers, we dreamers.*

The singing stops and Rosa gathers strands of webs into a little ball. She puts it into her weak eye. The tobacco has burnt itself out. She lights the cedar shavings. No fire, but sweet and piercing. She scatters the ground corn on the floor, tipping the rough clay bowl to its side, mingling the yellow with the cedar ash.

Her insight is blooming. It is becoming a way of seeing herself. Her life is not over. She has much to experience yet. She is getting older, but she is not old.

And some of the people were afraid to face the future and descended into the earth and became jointed: jet-black or red. These little ant people who live in the sand will also help you if you are lost.

She took the clay bowl and pressed it back into the cave wall.

For they also remember the time when we were one people.

Rosa stands and feels the darkness fall around her, but it is not from within, for she can see. Her white moon-eye, her shedded-snakeskin eye, her winter-worn-leaf eye: gone the thickening curtain, gone into the thoughts of the spider women. In and spin.

There are cedar trees floating in the air, and the faces of those she has loved waver delicately in front of her. She is seeing with her heart.

She feels the pain burning away. It's the pain of learning to let go. Sierra Rose is the name of the daughter she never had. Let go. Her husband's hands touching her in the morning. Let go. Her little son saying, "I'll always stay with you, Mama." Let go. Herself thinking: I'll never want another friend; they all leave or die and it hurts too much. Let go.

Her eye is clear. There is no division between the worlds of seeing and believing.

Rosa is ready to leave. She knows there is confusion outside and the noise of cars honking in the night. But there are also stars, one thousand billion of them in the Milky Way, and that leaves no room for self-pity. Rosa ties a lace on her Reeboks and turns around.

Those who stayed in the village grew taller as they taught their children how to face the future without fear.

She walks quickly toward the cave entrance, which has a lesser density of darkness. She passes the ancient paintings of red handprints and the pitted engravings of rayed suns. At the entrance itself, there are other human reminders: squashed beer cans, spray-painted initials, and an old McDonald's Coke cup. Golden arches. She sighs, then looks up. The moon is seeping out of the fat wheat heads. It's full and yellow, arching over the litter and the thin-winged twilight.

In the valley, she hears the cottonwoods shaking under the force of their water-filled roots. The bees are sleeping, dreaming of heavy black clouds booming over gold-white fields and sheet-lightning flashing into a hot and crinkly air.

And the ravens are dreaming of circling in a chicory-blue sky. Twirly seeds of yellow star-bursts fall in floating circles to the earth. Rosa feels the circles growing within her, as if she were a tree of immense dawn.

All of her life she's been drawn to the spirit, often equating contemplation with action. It takes energy to think, she'd tell herself. Now she knows why the phone never rang just because she was lonely. She has to get out and find something to do and someone to talk to!

Taking a deep breath, she smiles, thinking of her son and her new granddaughter. She'll give her a nickname: Sierra Rose. I'm not useless, she says firmly, and I'm not alone.

As she brushes the dirt from her clothes, she spares one last look at the cave. Its darkness, its blindness, had terrified her. It was the blindness of death she'd been seeing with her weak eye, the conception of nothing.

Now she begins the way back. In the distance, the sky is luminous with the lights of the city, and even though it may vaporize into thin air one day, if you are lost, you will know the way home; for home is a remembrance of when we were all one people.

And the people who live there are like enchanted trees, with bones for branches and eyes for leaves. If they listen, they can hear the humming of stars and bees and waves.

These are my ancestors, my future.

Note: While writing this story I developed a temporary eye infection. On a more significant level, writing this story convinced me that I wasn't too old to have another baby. My daughter, Maja Sierra Rose, was born when I was thirty-nine. Both she and my son, Aaron, are my future, but the past lives on in them in the blood and stories they've inherited from our ancestors.

Cortés Burning the Aviaries (acrylic, 1996)

Yaqui Deer Dancer (acrylic, 1998)

Coyote Spirit Ascending (watercolor, 1985)

Butterfly Woman (watercolor, 1986)

Waiting for the Bus to Guaymas (acrylic, 1998). In the background is Mount Tetakawi, or Stone Mountain in Yaqui. Closer, you can see the Yori Trailer Park ("white man's" trailer park), which was closed for business. My shadow is a deer.

On the Bus to Guaymas (acrylic, 1998). Look for the hidden deer. My friend, Lynette Copeland, who traveled with me, is getting on the bus behind the pelican.

Vicam Pueblo (acrylic, 1998). When we arrived in Vicam, it was almost Valentine's Day and the shops were covered with red paper valentines. My sister, Barbara, was supposed to travel with us, but at the last moment she couldn't find her birth certificate. I drew her in this painting in front center, along with myself in sunglasses and my daughter, Maja, next to me. Other family members are also represented since they were with me in spirit. Lynette can be seen taking photos in the center doorway. Can you see the other deer symbol?

The Family Tree

I was born Anita Louise Diaz in Long Beach, California. The following chart shows my ancestors, starting with my father, Alexander or Alex Diaz. Some of the names were spelled several ways, and no one knows for sure the correct way. For example, my grandfather was called Meetah, Emiterio, Emit, and Emiteria. Although many Yaquis changed their names to protect their Indian identity from Mexican authorities, it was also common to have several names throughout one's life.

The names also tell a bit of history. For example, Carlotta was the Mexicanized name of the Empress Charlotte (daughter of Leopold of Saxe-Coburg-Gotha), who married Maximilian, an Austrian Hapsburg who was appointed emperor of Mexico in 1864 by Napoleon. The emperor was later executed by Mexicans, and his empress died mentally unbalanced in Belgium in 1927. There were quite a few French soldiers stationed in the Guaymas area in the 1860s.

My mother believes that Carlotta was from Durango, Mexico, but we don't know whether she lived there temporarily or was born there. Durango was known for its silver and lead mines and commerce. Many Yaquis traveled to work in the mines all over northern Mexico and Arizona. Because Carlotta's father, Pedro Ramos, was a pack-train trader, and because she was well educated by Catholic nuns, I don't think her family worked as miners. After so many years, it's hard to find out what really happened. The Yaquis have been a mobile people during the last two hundred years.

Ancestors of Alexander Raymond Diaz

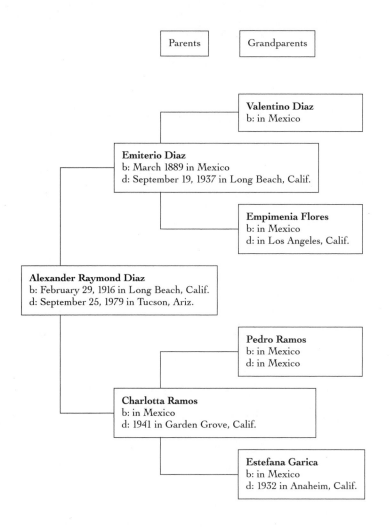

Parents | Grandparents

Valentino Diaz
b: in Mexico

Emiterio Diaz
b: March 1889 in Mexico
d: September 19, 1937 in Long Beach, Calif.

Empimenia Flores
b: in Mexico
d: in Los Angeles, Calif.

Alexander Raymond Diaz
b: February 29, 1916 in Long Beach, Calif.
d: September 25, 1979 in Tucson, Ariz.

Pedro Ramos
b: in Mexico
d: in Mexico

Charlotta Ramos
b: in Mexico
d: 1941 in Garden Grove, Calif.

Estefana Garica
b: in Mexico
d: 1932 in Anaheim, Calif.

Notes

Part One

The Gulf of California

1. The Yoemem, Yoremem, Kunkaak, and O-Otam were tribes who lived next to the Gulf of California.

The Female Soul of Mexico

1. The Spanish conquistadores used huge dogs to intimidate and kill natives. These dogs often weighed close to two hundred pounds. They were trained to maim, kill, and even devour native people, including children. Some conquistadores fed parts of native bodies to the dogs in order to accustom the dogs to human flesh. The famed "explorer" Balboa had a dog he called "Little Lion." It was part mastiff.

2. The quote is taken from the original text, which has been translated into English in modern times.

3. For more information about Our Lady of Guadalupe, see *Goddess of the Americas: Writings on the Virgin of Guadalupe*, edited by Ana Castillo (New York: Riverhead Books, 1996). Gloria Anzaldúa's article "Coatlalopeuh, She Who Has Dominion of Serpents," appears in this excellent book.

4. Malinche was a slave girl used by Cortés for sex and for her familiarity with native languages. She translated for him. She also bore him a son. In the past, she has been reviled, called a whore or a traitor. But she was a slave, without choice. Modern chicanas have redeemed her memory and honor her for her difficult life. She represents the birth of the mestizo, the modern Mexican race, which is both native and European in genetic heritage. She is the physical aspect of the Mother of Mexico.

5. For more information, read "Radiating in All Directions" in this book.

6. An excellent book on the contribution of native agriculture to the rest of the world is Jack Weatherford's *Indian Givers: How the Indians of the Americas Transformed the World* (New York: Crown Publishers, 1988).

Ceremony of Adoption of Orphaned Children

1. *Atole* is a gruel made from ground corn and boiled water, sometimes flavored with spices and other ingredients.

Part Two

Lost River

1. From the memories of Ben Wright, a Modoc survivor.

For Further Reading

If you would like to know more about the Yaquis, the following books may be helpful.

Choate, H. S. *The Yaquis: A Celebration*. San Francisco: Whitewing Press, 1997.

Giddings, Ruth Warner. *Yaqui Myths and Legends*. Tucson: University of Arizona Press, 1959.

Hu-DeHart, Evelyn. *Missionaries, Miners, and Indians: Spanish Contact with the Yaqui Nation of Northwestern New Spain, 1533-1820*. Tucson: University of Arizona Press, 1981.

Kaczkurkin, Mini Valenzuela. *Yoeme: Lore of the Arizona Yaqui People*. Tucson: Sun Tracks Press, University of Arizona, 1977.

Katz, Friedrich, ed. *Riot, Rebellion, and Revolution: Rural Social Conflict in Mexico*. Princeton, N.J.: Princeton University Press, 1988.

Kelley, Jane Holden. *Yaqui Women*. Lincoln: University of Nebraska Press, 1978.

Moisés, Rosalio. *Tall Candle: The Personal Chronicle of a Yaqui Indian*. Lincoln: University of Nebraska Press, 1977.

———. *A Yaqui Life*. Lincoln: University of Nebraska Press, 1971.

Molina, Felipe, and Larry Evers. *Yaqui Deer Songs / Maso Bwikam: A Native American Poetry*. Sun Tracks, vol. 14. Tucson: Sun Tracks and the University of Arizona Press, 1987.

Och, Joseph, S.J. *Missionary in Sonora: The Travel Reports of Joseph Och, S.J., 1755-1767*. San Francisco: California Historical Society, 1965.

Pérez de Ribas, Andrés. *History of the Triumphs of Our Holy Faith amongst the Most Barbarous and Fierce Peoples of the New World*. Ed. and trans. Daniel T. Reff, Maureen Ahern, and Richard K. Danford. Tucson: University of Arizona Press, 1999.

Sands, Kathleen. "The Singing Tree." *American Quarterly* 35 (1983): 355–75.

Savala, Refugio. *Autobiography of a Yaqui Poet*. Tucson: University of Arizona Press, 1980.

Spicer, Edward H. *Cycles of Conquest: The Impact of Spain, Mexico, and the United States on the Indians of the Southwest, 1533-1960*. Tucson: University of Arizona Press, 1962.

About the Author

Anita Endrezze is half Yaqui and half Romanian, German, Italian, and Slovenian. She is an artist as well as a writer, and her paintings have appeared on book covers and been exhibited in the United States, Great Britain, Finland, and Denmark. Her book of poems, *at the helm of twilight*, won both the 1992 Bumbershoot/Weyerhaeuser Award and the 1992 Governor's Writers Award for Washington State. Her most recent book, *The Humming of Stars and Bees and Waves* (Making Waves Press, 1998), is a collection of poetry and short stories. She has published extensively in anthologies and literary magazines in the United States and Europe; her work has been translated into five languages. A graduate of Eastern Washington University, she holds a Master of Arts degree from the Creative Writing Program. Married, with two children, she lives near Seattle.